Chuang-tzu
The Tao of Perfect Happiness

Books in the
SkyLight Illuminations Series

Chuang-tzu
The Tao of Perfect Happiness

Selections Annotated & Explained

Translation & Annotation
by Livia Kohn

Walking Together, Finding the Way ®
SKYLIGHT PATHS®
PUBLISHING
Woodstock, Vermont

Chuang-tzu:
The Tao of Perfect Happiness—Selections Annotated & Explained

2011 Quality Paperback Edition, First Printing
Translation, annotation, and introductory material © 2011 by Livia Kohn

For information regarding permission to reprint material from this book, please mail or fax your request in writing to SkyLight Paths Publishing, Permissions Department, at the address / fax number listed below, or e-mail your request to permissions@skylightpaths.com.

Library of Congress Cataloging-in-Publication Data
Zhuangzi.
  [Nanhua jing. English. Selections]
  Chuang-tzu : the Tao of Perfect Happiness : selections annotated & explained / translated & annotated by Livia Kohn. — Quality paperback ed.
    p. cm.
  Includes bibliographical references.
  ISBN 978-1-59473-296-6 (quality pbk.)
  I. Kohn, Livia, 1956- II. Title. III. Title: Tao of Perfect Happiness: selections annotated & explained.
  BL1900.C5E5 2011
  181'.114—dc22

2010046287

10   9   8   7   6   5   4   3   2   1
Manufactured in the United States of America
Cover design: Walter C. Bumford III, Stockton, Massachusetts
Cover art: Painted Butterfly—Illustration in Grunge Style © Freesurf #5633405 / fotolia.com

SkyLight Paths Publishing is creating a place where people of different spiritual traditions come together for challenge and inspiration, a place where we can help each other understand the mystery that lies at the heart of our existence.

SkyLight Paths sees both believers and seekers as a community that increasingly transcends traditional boundaries of religion and denomination—people wanting to learn from each other, *walking together, finding the way*®.

SkyLight Paths, "Walking Together, Finding the Way" and colophon are trademarks of LongHill Partners, Inc., registered in the U.S. Patent and Trademark Office.

Walking Together, Finding the Way®
Published by SkyLight Paths Publishing
A Division of LongHill Partners, Inc.
Sunset Farm Offices, Route 4, P.O. Box 237
Woodstock, VT 05091
Tel: (802) 457-4000   Fax: (802) 457-4004
www.skylightpaths.com

Contents ☐

Introduction □

The Chuang-tzu (Zhuangzi), named after its author, is the second major text of the Taoist (Daoist) tradition. It was compiled in the third century BCE and follows in the footsteps of the best-known and oldest of all Taoist texts, the Tao-te-ching (Daode jing; Book of the Tao and Its Potency), originally, like the Chuang-tzu, known by the name of its author, Lao-tzu (Laozi), which literally means "Old Master" or "Old Child."

Both works, rendered here in my own words, still form an active part not only of the Taoist tradition but also of Chinese culture in general. Read as classics, they are a must for every schoolchild, who can tell any number of stories from the Chuang-tzu and recite long passages from the Tao-te-ching. They are also at the core of Chinese literature, the Chuang-tzu being the first work of classical fiction with its numerous parables and fictional dialogues, the Tao-te-ching written in verse closely reminiscent of ancient poetry—as documented in the *Shih-ching* (*Shijing*), or Book of Songs—and thus one of the forerunners and main inspirations for Chinese poets. Both texts are also philosophical; they form the backbone of Taoism, constituting the root of an ancient and still actively pursued wisdom tradition that not only provides a bird's-eye view of how the universe functions but is also full of practical advice on how to live the best life—valid today as much as in the old days, possibly even more so.

There are many reasons to return to these ancient texts time and again, and especially to come back to the Chuang-tzu. The pure enjoyment of the stories, the vibrant humor of the tales, the fantastic aspects of reality—they all give pleasure, release, exuberance. The intricacies of ancient Chinese culture as revealed in the text, with its complex social hierarchies, demanding ways of interaction, extensive death rituals, and multiple layers of existence, from the creative power of "heaven" (a word indicating both the sky and the natural world at large) through gods and humans to animals and ghosts—they all spark interest, transcend present limitations, and open new ways of seeing and of being in the world. Last but not least, the complex philosophical and cosmological understanding of the universe, the vision of the individual as completely embedded in the greater flow of life, held and carried by the Way or Tao, the appreciation of the complete interconnectedness of all life, and the pervasive urging by the text to be who we are just as we are, no matter where we are—all these give power and inspiration, provide strength and determination, and encourage the will to live to the fullest.

With great admiration for and a deep delight in the text, I present the Chuang-tzu in this new reading with modern concepts and terms, hoping to bring the text not only to the minds but also to the hearts of people today. The translation reflects an understanding grown over three decades of deep involvement with Taoist studies (history, texts, concepts), spiritual practices (insight meditation, oblivion), and forms of body cultivation (diet, breathing, exercises). It is unique in that it selects passages by topic and makes ample use of the later chapters in the text, unlike previous translations that tend to follow the original order of chapters and focus especially on the first seven, called the "Inner Chapters" and certainly the oldest and best known. Without leaving them aside—and you will recognize many stories and arguments from them—this version places them in a thematic context, beginning with the core question of the text: "In this world, is there such a thing as perfect happiness?"

The answer, if you need to know now, is "certainly." But it takes work and a certain way of understanding self and reality combined with clear and persistent efforts to actualize this understanding in body and life—although, according to Chuang-tzu, these efforts are nowhere near as organized as later Taoists would propose. Over a total of fourteen chapters, the book then unravels key issues in Chuang-tzu's thought, from visions of the universe through understandings of fate, self, death, and dreams, to ways of personal transformation with the help of various forms of conscious reprogramming and meditative practice, which then lead to the best possible way of living in the world, exemplified in several different kinds of people and social situations.

Throughout, this book transliterates Chinese with the Wade-Giles system, developed by two sinological linguists from Britain in the late nineteenth century and still the foundation of the official transliteration system in Taiwan. In mainland China, it was superseded after the beginning of the People's Republic by a system called Pinyin, which is less linguistically sophisticated but simpler to read and easier to pronounce (and much easier to type!). Thus, the word for "way" is written *tao* in the old style and *dao* in the new, causing recent scholars to speak of Daoism rather than Taoism. Chuang-tzu—pronounced "Dshuwongdse"—comes out today as Zhuangzi. Pinyin is the way you will see Chinese personal and place-names in the newspaper; thus we now write Beijing for what used to be Peking, and Mao Zedong instead of the earlier Mao Tse-tung. Whenever you see no Pinyin in parentheses after a Wade-Giles name or term, either it has appeared previously or the two transliterations are in this particular case identical.

Historical Setting: A Period of Transition

The Chuang-tzu, like all other texts of ancient Chinese thought, arose in a period of economic and cultural change that transformed life and thought not only in China but also the world over. The German philosopher Karl Jaspers called this period the "axial age" in his seminal work *The Origin and Goal of History*. The term refers to the fact that at this time in many different cultures, new thinkers and religious leaders arose who, for the first time, placed great emphasis on the individual as opposed to the community of the clan or tribe. Examples include the Buddha in India, Zoroaster in Persia, Socrates in ancient Greece, and Confucius in China. The ideas proposed by these thinkers and religious leaders had a strong and pervasive impact on the thinking of humanity in general, contributing significantly to our thinking even today.

China at this time was undergoing tremendous economic and political changes. The arrival of iron-age technology, and with it better plow-shares, wagon axles, and weapons, had caused an increase in food production and massive population growth, as well as greater mobility and wealth among the people. This in turn led to a heightened hunger for power among local lords, who began to wage wars in order to expand their lands and increase their influence, setting large infantry armies against each other. While the central king of the Chou (Zhou) dynasty (1122–221 BCE) was still officially in charge of the entire country, there were in fact many independent states in a more or less constant state of conflict. The era is thus appropriately named the Warring States period. It was a time of unrest and transition, which left many people yearning for the peace and stability of old, and ended only with the violent conquest of all other states and the establishment of the Chinese empire by the Ch'in (Qin) dynasty in 221 BCE.

Most Chinese philosophers of the Warring States, in accordance with the situation they faced, were concerned with the proper "way" or "method" (*tao*) leading to the recovery of the harmony and social manageability of an earlier, golden age. Their works tend to be characterized by a strong backward focus and feudalistic vision. Although Western scholars usually characterize them as "philosophy," these texts always placed central emphasis on the practical dimensions of their teachings, both in regard to the individual's social behavior and to his or her personal self-cultivation. In fact, at the core of most ancient Chinese thought are practices of social discipline and the transformation of individuals and communities. Followers often congregated in small, almost sectarian groups rather than in what we think of as philosophical schools.

The earliest texts of Taoism are no exception. They are expressions of a tradition that in essence focused on practical and social transformation and can therefore be best understood within the wider context of the thought of the time. Later historians writing about the Warring States period after the fact, around 100 BCE, distinguished six major philosophical schools, each of which proposed one particular area as being most responsible for the state of social and cosmic disharmony and offered remedies accordingly: the Confucians focused on social etiquette and proper ritual; the Taoists emphasized the natural flow of things; the Mohists (named after the philosopher Mo-tzu [Mozi]) saw the solution to all problems in universal love; the Legalists thought that a set of strict laws and punishments was necessary to return order to the world; the Logicians found the key flaw in the inaccurate use of language and the resulting confusion in people's minds; and the Yin-Yang cosmologists understood social and personal harmony to depend on the cycles of the seasons, the movements of the stars, and other macrocosmic phenomena.

The Chuang-tzu, written when these schools were very much in evidence and had engaged in debates for several centuries, shows influence from all of them, in some cases supporting and integrating their views, in others strongly opposing them. In fact, the text as it has survived to the present day, abridged from its early version, contains materials above and beyond the philosophy of Chuang-tzu himself, whose thought is the main focus of this book.

The Chuang-tzu: A Text for Transformation

The Chuang-tzu takes its name from a minor government servant by the name of Chuang Chou (Zhuang Zhou, ca. 370–290 BCE). Highly erudite, he found officialdom useless and withdrew to dedicate himself to his speculations, teaching his ideas to disciples and inspiring them to write his teachings down. Early historical records mention that he was famous for his way with words. The literary mastery of the text is undisputed, and many consider it the first document of Chinese fiction.

The Chuang-tzu emerged from the same political environment as the Tao-te-ching but has a different focus in that it is more concerned with mental attitudes and condemns active political involvement. Chuang Chou found that the ongoing arguments among the different philosophical schools were futile and would not lead to serious improvements. He concluded that "right" and "wrong" were highly volatile categories, that all viewpoints were relative, and that the mind and its perception tended to be fallacious and one-sided. As a result, he makes a strong case for the cultivation of nondual perception and a way of life that is free from constraints—mental, personal, and social. To attain perfect happiness and harmony in life, he says, you need not become a sage; it is sufficient to free your mind and flow along smoothly with the course of Tao.

This philosophy makes up the bulk of the book, which consists of thirty-three chapters and is divided into three parts: Inner (1–7), Outer (8–22), and Miscellaneous (23–33). This tripartite division was established by the main commentator of the text, Kuo Hsiang (Guo Xiang), who lived in the third century CE (d. 312). Modern scholars divide the text slightly differently and note that it represents materials of four distinct strands of early Taoist thought: the school of Chuang Chou himself—in the Inner Chapters (also considered the oldest) and in chapters 16–27 and 32 of the later parts of the book—plus the so-called primitivists (chapters 8–10), the hedonists (chapters 28–31), and the syncretists (chapters 11–15, 33).

The primitivist chapters express a worldview very similar to that of the Tao-te-ching but are more radical in their demand for simplicity and the return to an uncomplicated life. They condemn all forms of culture and governance as evil and destructive and see the ideal society in terms of small communities that eschew all cultural and technological advances and live a simple life. Their idea is to keep people in one place as much as possible, to have them maintain a simple outlook on life and inner contentment by limiting their horizons of experience.

The hedonist strand diametrically opposes this. It promotes ease and leisure, a life of no constraints and no restrictions, an attitude of giving in to desires and serving only the individual's personal happiness and satisfaction. The underlying idea here is: "What is good for me is good for the universe." The reasoning behind it is that if the individual is part of Tao, then whatever he or she feels and wants is also part of Tao, and therefore all personal desires are expressions of the greater cosmic goodness and have to be satisfied without fail.

The syncretist sections of the Chuang-tzu, finally, demonstrate the integration of more formalized forms of cosmology and worldview into the basic understanding of Tao. Already the Tao-te-ching made a distinction between Tao as the creative, ineffable center and its manifestation in the visible world. Now the latter aspect of Tao is formulated in more technical detail and outlined in recognizable patterns. The rhythm of yin and yang is further subdivided into five phases (wood, fire, earth, metal, and water) and explained in complex cosmological correlations that also take into account observations of the natural world, the movements of the stars, and the divination of the I-ching (Yijing), the Book of Changes, a well-known classic of divination.

The Philosophy: Integrating Self and Universe

Chuang Chou rejects any entity or essence beyond natural life. For him, everything exists the way it is just because it is, in perfect spontaneity or naturalness. There is no principle or agency at the origin of life. There is only the underlying current, the continuous and all-encompassing flow of Tao, no ultimate cause beyond it that makes things what they are. The universe exists by itself and of itself; it is existence just as it is. Nothing can be added to or subtracted from it; it is entirely sufficient in itself.

People, like everything else, are part of the universal flow, of the spontaneous Tao and nature. Like all other entities, they arise and pass away, always in motion and constantly changing. Like all existing things, they have their particular inborn characteristics—their genetic makeup—and the position they are born in—their social circumstances and opportunities. These two, called essential nature and destiny, determine who people are in life. They are inescapable, just as the natural characteristic of change is in everything that is. Through them, Tao determines the particular way of being of the entire cosmos as much as of each individual.

The ideal way of being in the world, then, is to live as fully as possible in accordance with this personal Tao, the inner quality that determines the way people are. There is no point in trying to be something else. Nobody can ever comprehend what life is like for beings of a totally different size and dimension. The frog in the well has no concept of what it is like to live in an ocean. The little sparrow will never know what it is like to soar as a mighty eagle. Thus, freedom and ease in life do not come from wishing to attain one single goal that is the same for all—a high social position, advanced career, or scholarly erudition, for example—but from realizing who you are and where you stand in the world, from doing what you do best and to the fullest of your unique ability.

The problem with all this is that, despite their inborn Tao qualities, people develop consciousness and try to place themselves in relation to others and the world. They create ideals that do not match their inborn character or social standing, thus developing strife and fostering dissatisfaction. A good deal of Chuang-tzu's presentation accordingly focuses on how to overcome this consciously imposed limitation and recover perfect happiness.

One way Chuang-tzu suggests is to work with the conscious mind, to use critical awareness and analysis to realize just to what degree our perception is unreliable, how our evaluation of life and death, good and bad, desirable and undesirable depends on mental dualism and the faculty of divisive discrimination. It means realizing our tendency to split identity into many different selves by comparing ourselves with others and by making deliberate choices. There is a self that is richer than the next person, another self that is not as smart as someone else. There is a self that thinks it will live on and on, and there is yet another self that knows perfectly well that it will die. There is a division into this and that, into past and future, into mine and other. All these need to be recognized for what they are: artificial constructs that impede connection to spontaneity and happiness.

Overcoming this inherent tendency of the mind is achieved first of all through conscious questioning. How do we know that we know? How do we come to perceive that reality is what we think it is? What evidence is there that waking and dreaming are not the same thing? How do we know that life is not a great pain and death a wonderful rest? What, really, is my self?

The more we examine things from this perspective, the more we realize that there is ultimately no way of *really* knowing for sure who we are, where we come from, and where we are going. It is thus best to remain fully in the present with immediate attention and detached emotions, allowing the world to flow along through us, with us, and in us.

Beyond the conscious examination and elimination of categories, Chuang-tzu proposes several other methods to achieve perfect happiness. One is called "fasting of the mind": it activates *ch'i* (*qi*; vital energy), the subtle flowing force that connects all existence, over and above sensory perception. Another is "sitting in oblivion." This indicates a state of complete forgetfulness of self and other, high and low, life and death—the overcoming of all fears and concerns with dying and the otherworld—in a mind that is whole in itself and not concerned with classifying or evaluating the world either intellectually or emotionally.

A pervasively welcoming attitude toward all transformations, the ability to be at ease with the ongoing processes of the natural flow—often expressed with the word *t'ien* (*tian*), which means "sky" or "heaven"—this state of mind is the core of perfect happiness, the root of self-realization and a fulfilled life in the world. It is also the key characteristic of the ideal person: the sage or perfected. Such a person is free from strong feelings and opinions; at one with Tao or with the natural flow of "heaven," he or she is completely spontaneous and at ease with all that happens, living with a sense of strong immediacy that precludes thinking, evaluating, and critical mentation. The ideal way of being in the world for Chuang-tzu is, therefore, to be oblivious of conscious distinctions and evaluations, free from all liking and disliking, hope and fear, and to join heaven and earth in open-ended transformation.

A person who has reached this state can truly perfect his or her essential nature and will exhibit superior skills. The Chuang-tzu illustrates this in various cases of ordinary craftsmen who have mastered more than just their trade, such as Butcher Ting, who cuts up oxen with the same knife for years, or Woodworker Ch'ing, who makes bell-stands that seem out of this world. Other examples include a boatman who runs a ferry and a swimmer who instinctively moves with the waves. Both the boatman and the swimmer have a knack for the right way to handle themselves because they do not conceptualize their particular situations but act in the immediacy of life. Neither of them knows much consciously about his activities, but each moves naturally with his chosen element in oneness with his nature.

In all cases Tao works to the best of all in the perfection of naturalness or spontaneity. Naturalness is complete and happiness is perfect as and when the self is lost. The utter oblivion of the world in favor of a sense of flow in Tao, the ecstatic mental flight in free and easy wandering—that is ultimate realization in the Chuang-tzu, not only of Tao but also of the individual with his or her particular skills and in each particular life. Everyone, therefore, is originally happy and can live as a perfected person, whether in ordinary situations in the world or in a position of power.

Universal Patterns

1 This is the fundamental question of human existence: how to live in the world and attain a state of peace, contentment, and happiness. It has been discussed and written about innumerable times, from the ancient Greek philosophers through the Declaration of Independence to modern self-help manuals. Chuang-tzu provides his own set of answers to the question, and the entire book is really about nothing else: what constitutes happiness to begin with, how to go about attaining the ultimate state, and what life will look and feel like once it is reached. This is what this work is all about.

2 The way people of the world think of happiness is in terms of satisfying the five senses: seeing, hearing, smelling, tasting, and touching beautiful objects and gaining pleasure from them. But this is only a very limited way of attaining happiness, a momentary, fleeting sensation that leads to potential numbness. The Chuang-tzu and the Tao-te-ching have similar teachings: "The five colors make the eyes go blind; the five tones make the ears go deaf; the five flavors make the palate numb; racing and hunting cause the mind to run mad; rare objects create harm to one's activities" (Tao-te-ching chapter 12).

The text here sets the stage for distinguishing the joys of the senses from true happiness, which is independent of them.

1 □ Perfect Happiness

In this world, is there such a thing as perfect happiness? Is it possible to live to the fullest in this body? If so, what should we do? What can we rely on? What should we avoid, what support? What is best to pursue and what had better be abandoned? What should we delight in, what detest?[1]

The things people in today's world consider most valuable are wealth, position, vigor, and a sense of being good at something. The things that make them happy are physical comfort, rich tastes, beautiful clothes, lovely colors, and great music.

On the other hand, they uniformly detest poverty, low status, early death, and crime. Their greatest suffering occurs when their bodies cannot get comfortable, their mouths cannot feed on rich tastes, their physical form cannot fit into beautiful clothes, their eyes cannot look upon lovely colors, and their ears do not have a chance to listen to great music.

When they do not get these things, they are deeply frustrated and develop tremendous anxiety. Such utter dedication to their physical body—isn't this totally stupid?[2]

(continued on page 5)

3 Key goals of ordinary people, believed to create happiness, are wealth, position, and long life. All three make great demands on the body and tend to separate people from their authentic selves, preventing them from being fully vibrant and joyful in the present moment. People not only keep thinking of the future and developing all kinds of worries and anxieties, but they also define themselves through various achievements and are not really true to themselves.

4 The speaker here, possibly Chuang Chou himself, refrains from making value judgments. This again echoes the Tao-te-ching, where Lao-tzu says, "The sage has no ordinary mind, but makes the people's mind his own. The good, I treat good with goodness; the bad, I treat with equal goodness. Thus my inherent potency is full of goodness" (chapter 49). Yet he does assert that being competent and succeeding in the world will not provide happiness.

5 Wu Tzu-hsü (Zixu) was a minister in the feudal state of Wu. He repeatedly warned the king about a possible attack from a neighboring state, making "supportive suggestions" or "loyal remonstrations." His advice was not heeded, but his persistence aroused the king's anger.

He was ordered to commit suicide in 484 BCE. On the other hand, Wu became famous for presenting his convictions selflessly and without fear. Was that success? Was he happy? Should he have rather kept his mouth shut and lived safely but ignored?

Beyond questions of personal happiness, Chuang-tzu here raises issues that go to the heart of modern politics. Should dissenters keep quiet and safe or actively criticize and propose alternatives?

To attain wealth, people submit to great suffering and make themselves sick. Then they accumulate so much stuff that they cannot even use it! However dedicated they are to their lives, it is yet entirely outside of themselves.

To attain position, people slave day and night without stopping. Even then, they keep worrying constantly whether they come across as being good at their job! However dedicated they are to their lives, it is yet entirely separate from them.

When people are born, whatever they do, frustration is born along with them. Thus, even to attain long life, people make themselves ignorant and dull. Still, they spend all their time worrying about not dying. However dedicated they are to their lives, it is yet far away from them.[3]

Valiant fighters, all these people do lots of things to be seen as good at what they do by the world around them, yet they never really manage to live to the fullest. I do not know whether they are in fact good at what they do. But even if they are, that alone is not enough for them to live to the fullest. And if they are not, well, then they may just be living vicariously through others.[4]

Thus the advice: "If you make supportive suggestions that are not adopted, just sit still and let go. Do not push and compete."

Tzu-hsü pushed with his suggestions and got himself killed. Had he not pushed, he would not have become famous. So, was he good at living or not?[5]

People these days do all sorts of things and claim these make them happy, but I don't really know if they are in fact happy or not. I see how they go after their so-called happiness, pursuing it with the determination of death and as if unable to stop in their tracks. What they call happiness does not make sense to me, but then I can't really say it's not happiness either.

(continued on page 7)

6 Here the author first spells out his alternative: a sense of being in the world that is free from deficiency and strife, a feeling of completeness wherever you are and whatever you do. Happiness is so full in itself that it does not see itself as happy, a thought echoed in later Zen literature, which notes that it is quite impossible to ever know if one is enlightened. The ultimate state is just being in itself; it cannot be conceived as a separate entity or phenomenon. Any attempt to think about it or describe it necessitates its being separate, external, not just so. Similarly, accomplishment is fully realized when there is no more need for praise, reward, and completion. You just do what you do as you do it, and that is all.

7 The term the text uses to describe this state, in adaptation of the Tao-te-ching, is "nonaction" (*wu-wei*). This means developing a strong sense of self-identity, knowing what you can and cannot do, as well as an attitude of attunement to things around yourself. The ideal state is to flow along with inner and outer impulses in ongoing harmony, without making conscious decisions or striving for accomplishments.

8 The main argument for the possibility of such a mental state of perfect happiness is the way of nature, especially "heaven and earth"—a compound phrase that signifies the cosmos at large and indicates the various natural processes of life. Heaven is associated with yang energy; it is naturally light and bright and covers the world from above. Earth is made from yin energy; it is naturally solid and heavy and supports life from below. Neither has the conscious determination to be as it is; neither makes decisions, strives for accomplishments, or works hard. They just are what they are, doing what they do. Because of that, all else functions and the myriad things—all living, organic entities—take birth, grow, decline, and pass on.

Is there in fact happiness? Is it possible in this life and world? To me it is found only in complete nonaction, something that ordinary people see as great suffering. Thus the saying: "Perfect happiness is being free from the need to be happy. Perfect accomplishment is being free from having to accomplish anything."[6]

What is right and wrong in the world is impossible to decide. However, in nonaction there is clear right and wrong. Perfect happiness and living to the fullest can only be realized in this state of nonaction.[7]

Let me explain this a bit more. Heaven rests in nonaction and is perfectly luminous. Earth rests in nonaction and is perfectly at peace. As these two merge in their respective states of nonaction, the myriad things come forth.[8]

How vast! How amazing! They seem to come from nowhere. How amazing! How vast! They have no image or symbol.

The myriad things in their great variety all grow from cosmic nonaction. Thus the saying: "Heaven and earth rest in nonaction and there is nothing that they do not do."

What, then, can a mere human being do to attain this ultimate state of nonaction?

—CHAPTER 18

9 Outlining the typical problems of ordinary people in more detail, this section describes the ways of people who are seen as successful, yet shows how they are not really the path to perfect happiness.

You commonly covet good looks, a great body, and an outgoing, alpha personality as the gate to admiration and success, the means by which you can get ahead in the world and reach the higher rungs of achievement. However, they lead to great involvement and concerns, thus preventing a focus on what is really important to you deep within.

By the same token, to get ahead in the existing social and corporate structures, you have to follow current fashions, bend with the winds of time, be subservient and compliant with whatever orders are being handed down from above. Again, you are moving further away from being true to yourself.

Then there are those various internal virtues commonly seen as signs of a great personality and positive integrity, such as wisdom, courage, and thinking of others (such as the Confucian values of benevolence and righteousness). In Chuang-tzu's view, they do nothing but add to your burdens, hindering your pursuit of long life and preventing you from finding perfect harmony and happiness in your unique life on the planet.

Trouble has eight signs; success has three needs; the body has six problem areas.

A beautiful face, great hair, tall stature, good muscle tone, vigor, style, courage, and chutzpah—when someone has these eight more than others, they bring nothing but trouble.

Following the current fashion, leaning and bending, abject and subservient—when someone acts like this more so than others, he or she will find success in the world.

Wisdom and insight lead to outside involvement; courage and enterprise lead to numerous resentments; benevolence and righteousness lead to piles of responsibility—thus these six create problems for the body.[9]

—CHAPTER 32

10 Moderation is the ideal described in antiquity as well as in Taoist texts from an early period: avoid all overindulgence in food and drink as well as in all sorts of sensual and sexual pleasures and instead observe guidelines for healthy living. The medieval *Yang-sheng-lun* (On Nourishing Life) proposes six:

1. Let go of fame and profit.

2. Limit sights and sounds.

3. Moderate material goods and wealth.

4. Lessen smells and tastes.

5. Eliminate lies and falsehood.

6. Avoid jealousy and envy.

11 Chuang-tzu here paints a terrible picture of what an excess of wealth and material goods does to people: not a moment's peace due to excessive sensory exposure to sounds and sights, constantly buffeted by passions and desires for yet more stuff, always running after the next project and greater profits, and suffocating in all their possessions and in the multiple houses and storage facilities needed to maintain them.

People who live a life of excess suffer greatly—they are sick with longing, overburdened by stuff, and constantly fearful that someone will cheat or rob them. What a terrible way to live!

Moderation brings good fortune; excess causes harm—this holds true for every being and all kinds of situations but especially in the case of wealth.[10]

Look at the wealthy: their ears are overwhelmed by the sounds of rock and pop, blues and rap; their mouths are filled with meat and wine. These rouse their intention for more of the same so they completely forget their real position in the greater scheme of things—this is confusion.

Drowning in surging energies and passions, they are like laborers lugging an uphill burden—this is suffering.

Amassing material goods, they try to find comfort; amassing power and influence, they try to find fulfillment. Resting quietly for a moment, they sink into depression; engaging themselves physically, they turn into maniacs—this is sickness.

Pursuing wealth and running after profit, they fill their houses to overflowing and do not know how to escape. Still, they lust for more and cannot resist—this is addiction.

More stuff piled up than they could ever use, grasping for more than they could ever hold, their mind is full of care and close to exhaustion, yet they still keep going after projects and things, not knowing when to stop—this is trouble.

At home suspicious of theft by deceitful servants, in town terrified of attacks by robbers and con artists, they surround themselves with alarm systems in their houses and dare not walk around by themselves outside—this is fear.

These six—confusion, suffering, sickness, addiction, trouble, and fear—are the greatest evils in the world.[11]

—CHAPTER 29

12 Look, on the other hand, at the happiness of the frog in the well. Chuang-tzu often illustrates his point with parables—typically featuring animals, mythical heroes, and sage emperors, or well-known political and philosophical figures such as Confucius. Here he describes the frog in a tiny, old, and crumbling well who is as happy as he could possibly be, having found his true calling in life and not needing anything extraneous or fancy to give him fulfillment.

13 In contrast to the frog, a small creature with a limited horizon, the turtle of the Eastern Sea is a huge beast in a vast ocean who needs a completely different habitat to find self-realization. Each is happy in its own way and would be completely at odds in the other's setting. The poor frog is flabbergasted to learn about the vastness of the sea; the poor turtle can't even get a foot into the tiny well. They cannot really understand the other's habitat and "happiness." But that is exactly the point: there is perfect happiness for each of us if we just take the trouble of looking within and finding our very own perfect habitat and way of life.

14 A *li* is a Chinese mile, about 440 meters—about a quarter mile or a bit less than half a kilometer.

15 Emperor Yü was the founder of the Hsia (Xia) dynasty (ca. 2000–1700 BCE), known as the tamer of the floods, who opened channels to allow the water to flow into the sea, which yet did not change its inherent nature despite the excess.

16 King T'ang was the founder of the Shang dynasty (1766–1122 BCE), best known for ancestor worship, oracle bone divination, and bronze vessels. The country suffered from extensive drought, and the king exposed himself to the heat to make heaven take pity and provide rain. Yet the cliffs were unaffected by the excess, resting firmly in their true so-being.

There once was a frog who lived in a crumbling well. He said to the turtle of the Eastern Sea, "I am so happy! I hop out of the well and sit on the rim. I jump into the well and rest on its broken tiles. I move around in the water, drawing my legs together and lifting my chin. I squirrel into the mud, diving until my feet are all sunk. I turn around, seeing the friendly shrimps, crabs, and tadpoles. How could I suffer in this wonderful life? More than that, I have complete command over the water in the gully and utter freedom of movement all over the crumbling well. This is perfection! Hey, Master Turtle, why don't you come over and join me and see for yourself?"[12]

The turtle of the Eastern Sea had not even put his left foot into the well when his right knee caught and got stuck.[13] He hesitated and drew back, then proceeded to tell the frog about the sea:

"A distance of a thousand *li* does not describe how big it is.[14] A height of a thousand aligned swords does not approach its depth. In the time of Emperor Yü, they had floods for nine years out of ten, yet its water did not rise.[15] Under King T'ang, there was a drought for seven years out of eight, yet its cliffs did neither extend nor shrink.[16] To be unaffected by short- or long-term changes, to be immune to increase or decrease of whatever amount—this is the great happiness of the Eastern Sea."

When the well frog heard this, he was startled and scared. Completely bewildered, he didn't know anymore who he was.

—CHAPTER 17

17 This story from chapter 17 reiterates the same idea as the dialogue between the well frog and the ocean turtle. The P'eng, a huge fish transformed into a gigantic bird, rises vastly over the ocean and moves with ease from the Northern to the Southern seas. The cicada and the little dove, on the other hand, barely make it to the nearest treetop. Each of them is unique; each is happy in its own way. Yet neither can really understand the other or could take the other's place.

Matching Confucian and other traditional Chinese thought, Chuang-tzu here sees no equality in the sense that anyone could do anything in society or is equally capable of filling certain positions. On the other hand, he champions equality in the sense that everyone has his or her own unique talents and special place in the greater scheme of things. Society should make sure that each person has an equal chance at fully developing his or her unique potential and finding a particular form of happiness—be it jumping around like the frog in the well or rising on the whirlwind like the great P'eng.

18 This paragraph puts the matter in a practical way: different journeys require different forms of provisioning, but none is better than the other. It would be wrong and harmful to take three-day provisions on a month-long trip or to carry tons of food for a short outing to the park. Yet this is exactly what people do when they strive for wealth and position and all those other goals society sets before them. They orient themselves outside and blatantly disregard their own innate abilities (essential nature) and social context (original destiny), factors that both set limits and open undreamed-of opportunities.

19 P'eng-tsu (Pengzu) lived for eight hundred years without aging. He practiced the arts of nourishing life, including breathing techniques, healing exercises, and meditations, and lived on fruits, herbs, minerals, and powdered deer antlers. Asked to serve as an official under the legendary Chou dynasty ruler King Mu, he refused but offered his sagely teachings. But that was his way—it is not for everyone. We all have to find our own unique way in the world.

In the Northern Sea lives a fish known as K'un, which is huge—I don't know how many *li*. It changes into a bird called P'eng, whose back is also big—I don't know how many *li*. When this bird stirs and rises up in flight, its wings cover the entire sky like clouds. On occasion, the sea changes its tides. Then the bird migrates to the Southern Sea, also known as the Celestial Lake.

The Universal Harmony, a book on wondrous feats, notes: "When the P'eng migrates to the Southern Sea, it strikes the water over a surface of three thousand *li*, then lifts on the whirlwind to a height of ninety thousand *li*, and comes to rest only after half a year has passed."...

A cicada and a little dove laugh at him. "We fly with effort, hoping to land on an elm or a sapanwood. Sometimes we don't even make that and fall back down before we reach it. How could anyone ever rise to ninety thousand *li* and make for the south?"[17]

If you go on a short excursion to the blue yonder, you take provisions for three meals and return just as full. If you go on a hundred-*li* journey, you need to pound grain when you stop for the night. If you travel as far as a thousand *li*, you need to carry provisions for three months.[18]

What do these two critters know? Small knowledge reaches nowhere near great knowledge; a few years' experience does not match that of many years. How do we know this? The mushroom that lives only for a morning has no idea of the phases of the moon. The cicada who lives only for a few days does not know the seasons of spring and fall. These are examples for short-lived creatures.

On the other end of the spectrum, there is a numinous creature in the southern state of Ch'u, whose spring and fall last five hundred years each. In the old days, there was the great Ch'un tree, whose spring and fall lasted eight thousand years each. The immortal P'eng-tsu, moreover, is known for his extraordinary length of life. Now lots of ordinary people try to match him. How pitiful, indeed![19]

—CHAPTER 17

1 This section raises the question why, if the universe is ultimately perfect and all beings have an ideal way of being and a perfect niche in the world that is suited uniquely to them, there is so much unhappiness and confusion. It connects the question immediately to issues of mental classification and verbal expression, the development of human consciousness and its various manifestations.

2 In Chuang-tzu's time, there were six major philosophical schools, which each proposed one particular area as being most responsible for the state of social and cosmic disharmony and offered remedies accordingly: the Confucians focused on social etiquette and proper ritual; the Taoists emphasized the natural flow of things; the Mohists (named after the philosopher Mo-tzu) saw the solution to all problems in universal love; the Legalists thought that a set of strict laws and punishments was necessary to return order to the world; the Logicians found the key flaw in the inaccurate use of language and the resulting confusion in people's minds; and the Yin-Yang cosmologists understood social and personal harmony to depend on the cycles of the seasons, the movements of the stars, and other macrocosmic phenomena.

3 To begin unraveling the different perspectives and liberate the mind from the classifications that put limitations on concepts and experience, Chuang-tzu advocates that we realize how everything in our thinking depends on categories of this and that, right and wrong, good and bad, like and dislike. We will never be truly free and genuinely happy as long as we cling to these evaluative patterns.

2 □ The Universe

How, then, has this state come about, that the original inherent way of being—the Tao—is now so obscure that it is classified according to true and false? How has human speech become so obscure that it is classified according to right and wrong? Is it that Tao has gone off and is no longer there? That speech is there but not really valid?[1]

Tao is obscured by partial accomplishments; speech is obscured by flowery language. Thus we now have the contentions of different philosophical schools—one saying "right" where the other says "wrong," and vice versa.[2] To decide on what is actually right and what is in fact wrong, it is best to shine an impartial light on things.

All things have a "this" and a "that." Looking at them only from the perspective of "this," we can't really see them for what they are, and only by knowing them as they really are can we understand them. Realize: all "this" arises from "that," and all "that" follows "this." "This" and "that" are interdependent and co-originating: as one arises, the other ends, and as one ends, the other arises; as one is acceptable, the other becomes unacceptable, and as one is unacceptable, the other becomes acceptable. Thus, "this" and "that" are intimately connected, and "right" and "wrong" depend on each other.[3]

—CHAPTER 2

4　In more cosmic terms, the beginning of the problem rests with the fundamental human constitution of having sensory faculties and relating to the world through them. This is expressed most vividly in the creation myth concerning Hun-tun, which in Cantonese is pronounced "wonton" and is still popular in the soup of this name. Described as a formless sack or unshaped bulk of energy, the figure here is the ruler of the center.

5　Although he is without sensory faculties, Hun-tun is generous and kind, hosting his neighbors with enthusiasm. To repay his kindness, they try to make him more like other creatures and drill sensory openings into him—as a result of which Hun-tun dies. He is, as Norman Girardot says in *Myth and Meaning in Early Taoism*, "bored to death."

The point of the story, then, is that the state of inherent wholeness, of the oneness with Tao we are originally born with, is destroyed bit by bit the more we use the senses to relate to the world. On their basis we develop likes and dislikes and start to use our conscious mind to separate ourselves from reality, evaluating sensory data in terms of good and bad, high and low, advantageous and detrimental, and so on.

The point of the Chuang-tzu's program of return to perfect happiness—and the goal of all Taoist mysticism and practice over the ages—is the recovery of this state of original chaos, of oneness with Tao, of wholeness within.

The ruler over the Southern Sea was Shu [Tight]. The ruler over the Northern Sea was Hu [Abrupt]. The ruler over the center was Hun-tun (Hundun) [Chaos].[4]

On occasion Shu and Hu would meet in the realm of Hun-tun, who received them with great hospitality. The two then started to plan how they could possibly pay back Hun-tun's kindness.

They said, "All people have seven orifices so they can see, hear, eat, and breathe. He alone has none of them. Let us try boring him some."

So they bored a hole every day, and on the seventh day Hun-tun died.[5]

—CHAPTER 7

6 One way of understanding how sensory evaluation works is in terms of classical Chinese cosmology, which sees the origin and development of the universe in terms of the two complementary forces yin and yang. Originally geographical terms that indicated the sunny and shady sides of a hill, they acquired a series of associations: bright and dark, light and heavy, strong and weak, above and below, heaven and earth, ruler and subject, male and female, and so on.

They arose at the time of creation, after unformed chaos gave rise to cosmic oneness, which in turn separated into the two fundamental energies: yang as the active, moving, and outgoing force, and yin as the restorative, calming, and inward-moving tendency. They spiraled away from each other, lighter yang rising up to form the sky or heaven and heavier yin sinking down to form the land or earth. From there they continued to intermingle and gave rise to all beings, who continue to be constituted by yin and yang parts.

The two forces closely depend on each other; one cannot be present without the other, as is aptly shown in the classic yin-yang diagram, which clearly shows the balance and interlocking nature of yin and yang, the fluidity of their interchange.

Still, while we can observe their patterns, we can never quite understand why they work in this manner and how they come about.

In a state of high yin, all is cold and severe; in a state of high yang, all is turbulent and agitated. Coldness and severity come from heaven; turbulence and agitation issue from earth. When both intermingle and join, all things come forth.

You may try to see some order in all this, but you will never be able to see its ultimate form. Growth and decay, fullness and emptiness, darkness and light, solar and lunar phases—they all are new every day, yet you will never be able to see how they work exactly.

Life has a point from which it springs; death has a point to which it returns. Beginning and end succeed each other without obvious turning points, and no one knows what possible limits they may have. If it is not an ongoing process like this, then who runs this whole shebang?[6]

—CHAPTER 21

7 A way of looking at conscious, critical evaluation of the world is in terms of intellectual speculation. Any theory, any logical argument, when taken far enough, will be just speculation. There is ultimately no way of really knowing what in fact exists or is being said. As the commentator Kuo Hsiang explains:

> What existed before there were beings? If I say yin and yang were first, then that means yin and yang are beings, too. What, then, was before them? I may say nature was first. But nature is only the natural way of beings. I may say perfect Tao was first. But perfect Tao is perfect nonbeing. Since it is nonbeing, how can it be before anything else? So, what existed before there were beings? There must always be another thing being without end.

He comes to the conclusion that "beings are what they are by nature; they are not caused by anything else," reaching a state of pure acceptance (like Hun-tun) that both precedes and goes beyond classifications.

8 Chuang-tzu takes it one step further and introduces a paradox: something known to be tiny (a tip of a hair) is described as big, while something known as big (Mount T'ai) is classified as tiny. He shows here that all evaluations in terms of size or longevity or anything else are mere conventions with no solid reality to them.

9 Ultimately, all beings and all existence are one, but speech and consciousness create distinctions. They do not stop with one distinction, either, but immediately move into innumerable divisions and classifications, getting further and further away from ultimate reality.

There is a beginning. There was a beginning before that beginning. There was a beginning before that beginning before there was the beginning.

There is existence. There was nonexistence before that. There was existence before the beginning of that nonexistence. There was nonexistence before the existence before nonexistence.

So, if now there suddenly is nonexistence, how do we know whether it is in fact existence or actually nonexistence?

Now I have just said something, but how do I not know if I have in fact said something or if I haven't really said anything?[7]

In the world there is nothing greater than the tip of a hair, and the great Mount T'ai is tiny. There is none longer lived than a dying infant, and the immortal P'eng-tsu had a short life.[8]

Heaven, earth, and I came along together, and the myriad things and I are one. Since we are all one, how can I ever talk about them? Since I am talking about them, how can there be no talk?

Myself and my talking make two; talking and the object make three. Moving on from here, even the best mathematician cannot count them all—how much less can ordinary people?[9]

So, coming from nonexistence and moving to existence, we get to three. Coming from existence and moving to more existence, we get to how many? There is no point going anywhere without understanding the interdependence of "this" and "that."

—CHAPTER 2

10 A later chapter takes up this tendency of classification, using the same basic imagery (a tiny hair versus a great landscape), and expresses it in a fictional dialogue of two divinities—the local River God and the expansive Lord of the Northern Sea.

11 You should realize four things about reality to remedy your inherent tendency toward classification: there is no limitation to existence and even minute things can be very significant; there is no stopping of time and thus no point in feeling sorry about the past or trying to hang on to the present; there is no control over what happens in life, and all emotions are just so much wasted energy; and there is no great universal reason for being on the planet, so that all interpretations and reactions to life and death are ultimately futile.

In other words, develop a conscious perspective that releases evaluations even of momentous things, such as life and death, combined with a change in emotions to a more accepting attitude. This will help you attain inner peace and open the way to true happiness.

12 Another important part of this is to see things from a larger perspective: whatever we know is nowhere near the total amount of knowledge on the planet; compared to the course of history or, even worse, the millions of years of galactic unfolding, our life span is but a tiny moment. We can be content with what we have and what we can do—trying to reach out far beyond will only lead to frustration.

The River God said, "Now, is it all right if I think of heaven and earth as big, and the point of a hair as small?"[10]

The Lord of the Northern Sea replied, "No. When it comes to things, measure is without limit; time is without end; allotment is without constancy; and beginning and end are without cause.

"For this reason, if you observe all that is near and far with great understanding, you see something small yet do not think it insignificant, find something big yet do not think it important. This is how you realize that the measure of all things is without limit.

"If you objectively witness all that is old and new, you look at the past yet do not feel regret, touch the present yet do not stretch to reach it. This is how you realize that time is without end.

"If you examine all that is full and empty, you succeed in something yet do not feel great joy, fail in something yet do not get frustrated. This is how you realize that allotment is without constancy.

"If you shed a bright light on all that is coming and going, you come to life yet do not celebrate, face death yet do not find it disastrous. This is how you realize that beginning and end are without cause.[11]

"Whatever people know is nowhere near the amount they don't know; the time they spend on the planet is nowhere near the time they are not around. Trying to pursue the ultimately large with the totally tiny only leads to error and confusion—this way you never find self-realization![12]

"Seen from this perspective, how can you know that the point of a hair is sufficient to determine what is small or that heaven and earth give you any indication of what is big?"

—CHAPTER 17

13 How, then, did people come to even try to move beyond their sphere? As an explanation, the Chuang-tzu outlines four stages that saw the development of culture and the establishment of classificatory consciousness. Kuo Hsiang explains them as follows:

1. Chaos Complete: This is the state of complete oblivion of heaven and earth, of total abandonment of the myriad beings. Outside never examining time and space, inside never conscious of the body. Thus people are boundless and free from all fetters, they go along with beings and are in full accordance with all.

2. Beings: Even though oblivion is no longer complete now and beings are recognized as existing, there is still the oblivion of distinctions between this and that.

3. Distinctions: At this stage, there is a distinction between this and that for the first time. However, there are no evaluations in terms of right and wrong.

4. Right and Wrong: If [the distinction between] right and wrong were not there, Tao would still be complete. With the destruction of Tao, emotions begin to be partial and love develops. As long as you cannot forget one-sided love and free yourself from egotism, there is no way you can ever find original oneness in yourself or with others.

However, Chuang-tzu concludes the presentation by asking if any of this is actually real or whether the entire vision of purity, development, and decline is not yet another make-believe construct of the human mind. The core idea, whether expressed in stages or not, is the need to step back from all classifications.

People of old had perfect knowledge. How was it "perfect"? They thought in a way that matched the stage before things existed. Their knowledge was perfect and exhaustive; nothing could possibly be added to it.

Next, they saw things as existing, yet they did not yet make any distinctions among them.

Then a stage came when people made distinctions among things, but they had as yet no sense of right and wrong.

When right and wrong began to appear in people's minds, the Tao was destroyed. The destruction of the Tao, then, meant the beginning of personal preference and one-sided love.

Yet, is there really something we can call destruction and accomplishment? Or are there ultimately none of these?[13]

—CHAPTER 2

14 The development of consciousness comes with concrete changes in lifestyle and culture. In the very earliest phases of human development, what we would call the Paleolithic, people were hunter-gatherers and lived in trees or caves, trying to stay away from the vast numbers of roaming predators. They had little sense of being different from other creatures, and their consciousness was tribal and undifferentiated.

In the next stage of development, humans learned to harness the power of fire. They could hunt animals and cook their meat; they could also gather firewood and burn it. At this point they had awareness of the changing seasons and started to plan ahead for the cold times to come—losing a bit of their original "oblivion" while gaining comfort and security.

15 From here culture developed with various key feats. Agriculture, what we would call the Neolithic Revolution, allowed people to control their food supply and establish matrilineal clans, but they still lived in small communities, and there was enough to go around. Then scarcity appeared and there were the first wars, notably nomadic groups raiding settled cities, as is well known from the Near East and India. After that, more complex institutions evolved, with extensive bureaucracies and governmental control—to the point of injustice and misery that have characterized most of history.

The Chinese express this development in terms of "culture heroes": the Divine Farmer who developed agriculture; the Yellow Emperor, who fought the first war, created infrastructure, and established markets; the Confucian epitomes Yao and Shun, who organized the government; and the founders of the first dynasties, who came to the throne by forcefully removing previous rulers. For the Chuang-tzu, they didn't do too well, since so-called civilization is nothing more than an organized structure of bullying and exploitation.

I have heard that in the most ancient of times birds and beasts were numerous while human beings were few. So the people all built nests in trees to avoid them. During the day they gathered acorns and chestnuts; at night they climbed back up to the top of the trees. For this reason they are called the people of the nesting clan.

Following this, in high antiquity, people knew nothing about clothes and garments. In the summertime they would collect great piles of firewood, which they would then burn in the winter to keep warm. For this reason they are called the people who knew how to live.[14]

In the age of the Divine Farmer, the people slept in peace at night and got up to proceed with calm. They knew their mothers but not their fathers, and they lived side by side with the elk and the deer. They tilled the soil to eat, wove fabrics to dress themselves, and in their hearts and minds were utterly free from ideas of doing each other harm. This is the epitome of perfect potency.

However, the Yellow Emperor could not reach this level. He fought the battle of Cho-lu (Zhuolu) against the Wormy Rebel, and the blood flowed for a hundred *li*. Then Yao and Shun arose and established innumerable offices. King T'ang removed his overlord; King Wu killed the old ruler. Ever since, the strong have been bullying the weak, the many have been exploiting the few. From T'ang and Wu onwards, those in power have been a band of criminals and nothing more.[15]

—CHAPTER 29

16 Compared to the plight of humanity in "civilized" societies, animals are closer to original Chaos and have a much better life: they don't mind a thing as long as they are in an environment that supports their basic needs. They maintain an internal constancy of mind and heart that is not touched by emotions nor affected by mental classifications.

17 This is the goal: realizing ultimate oneness not just by conscious understanding but in the core of your very being; getting to a point where the body is just part of the greater life on earth; feeling at a deep level that life and death are part of the same continuum and make no more difference than the changes of day and night. Then there are no more disturbances to inner peace and stability, and you can live in perfect happiness.

Grass-eaters do not mind changing pastures; river creatures do not worry about changing waters. They can make small changes without ever losing their great constancy; joy and anger, sadness and delight do not enter into their breasts.[16]

Now, in that they all live in the world, the myriad things are one. Realizing that they are ultimately all part of overarching oneness, their four limbs and hundred body parts are just so much dust and dirt to them, and all life and death, all beginning and end, are just like the succession of day and night: none of it can disturb them.[17] How much less will they be bothered by the gain and loss, disaster and good fortune of ordinary life?

—Chapter 21

1 How, then, do we go about getting to this ideal state? The first step is to realize that the entire universe, and thus also our own body and mind, our life and death, are nothing but vital energy (*ch'i*). In ancient sources associated with mist, fog, and moving clouds, the word consists of an image of someone eating and grain in a pot. *Ch'i* is thus the quality that nourishes, warms, and transforms as well as anything perceptible but intangible: atmosphere, smoke, aroma, vapor, a sense of intuition, foreboding, or even ghosts.

There is only one *ch'i*, just as there is only one Tao. But it appears on different levels, most importantly primordial *ch'i*, which we receive from heaven through our parents, and postnatal *ch'i*, which we get from the environment through breath, food, and interaction with others. All existence is nothing but *ch'i*, which flows continuously in a rhythm of yin and yang and should be smooth, even, and ever changing.

2 On the other hand, any excess or deficiency in the flow, in the inherent transformation pattern, is a form of disturbance that manifests as disease. Seeing things as good and bad, spiritual and putrid, and whining about them, then, is a basic form of imbalance that keeps you from realizing your true nature and causes not only discontent but also disease.

3 The countermeasure is to use the concept of *ch'i* to realize the fundamental oneness of all existence and stop seeing yourself as separate. This, then, will also allow you to see death as part of the continuous flow of existence.

3 □ Life and Death

Life is the follower of death, and death is the beginning of life—who knows their inherent structure?

Human life is nothing but an assemblance of vital energy. When it comes together, we come to life; when it scatters, we die.[1] Since life and death thus closely follow each other, why whine about either?

In this most essential aspect, the myriad things are one. They consider life as beautiful because it is spiritual and marvelous; they think of death as nasty because it is smelly and putrid.

However, the smelly and putrid change again and become the spiritual and marvelous; the spiritual and marvelous change once more and turn smelly and putrid.[2]

Thus the saying: "The entire world is but one vital energy." Based on this, all sages value oneness.[3]

—Chapter 22

4 | Another way to counteract the tendency to "whine" about death is to ask whether we really know what happens after we die. Or, as the Chuang-tzu says in chapter 2, "How do we know that loving life is not a delusion? That hating death is not being like someone who has lost his way and cannot find his home?"

The skull story is a case in point. It was highly unusual to find human remains by the roadside in traditional China, where people had to be buried with all the proper rites to make sure they arrived safely in the otherworld and could receive appropriate offerings and not bother the living for sustenance or attention. The reasons the Chuang-tzu lists here are all possible causes for not dying properly, in the arms of the person's kin—different ways of being cast out, which, according to classical belief, also means a particularly nasty and unsettled existence in the otherworld.

5 | Despite his outcast status, the skull asserts that life after death is great fun and a form of perfect happiness—the kind of happiness we pursue all our life (harmony, equality, prosperity)—and means the end of toil without the loss of identity or the ability to feel. It is not a fall into some deep abyss; it is not a shadow existence; it is not a form of punishment or deprivation. On the contrary, it is like coming back to "our true home," the way we really should be, calm and peaceful, equitable and relaxed, a state to be aspired to even during life—and most certainly not feared.

Chuang-tzu once went to the state of Ch'u. On the road he found a hollow skull, bleached out but still clearly retaining a skull shape. He tapped it with his horsewhip and started talking to it:

"Did you end up here because you were so greedy for life that you lost your mind? Perhaps you betrayed your country and suffered capital punishment or exposure in the wilderness? Did you die all alone because you behaved unethically, disgracing your parents, wife, and children? Did you freeze or starve to death on the road? Or did you just die a natural death at the end of your allotted time?"[4]

Having voiced his speculations, Chuang-tzu moved the skull to the roadside, used it for a pillow, and went to sleep. In the middle of the night, the skull appeared to him in a dream. It started talking:

"You were finding causes there quite like the great disputer! Yet look at what you said: it's all about stuff of interest only to the living. In death, none of this is relevant. Would you like to hear about the joys of being dead?"

"Yes, indeed, very much so."

"In death," the skull explained, "there is no ruler above, no subject below. Nor is there any seasonal or other change. Equitably, we take heaven and earth for our spring and autumn. Even if you were a king facing south on his throne, you wouldn't have it any better."

Chuang-tzu did not believe him. "Let's see," he said. "Suppose I got the Ruler of Destiny to bring you back to life and give you a healthy body with bones and flesh, sinews and skin, plus return you to your father and mother, wife and children, and all your local friends, wouldn't you want that?"

Hearing this, the skull gazed at him deeply, knitted its brow, and replied, "You must be kidding! Why in the world would I give up the happiness of a king facing south and again subject myself to the toils of human life?"[5]

—CHAPTER 18

6 In concrete reality, this advanced attitude toward death finds expression in the behavior of mourners. In traditional China, immediate relatives (spouses, children) had to mourn for a full three years— rough clothes, few baths, plain food, no work, and certainly no entertainment—and at the funeral show their grief vividly by wearing sackcloth and ashes, exhibiting disheveled hair and appearance, and wailing and crying loudly. There are even professional mourners who can be hired to enhance the atmosphere of sadness and grief, to make sure that everyone knows how harsh the break of social continuity is for the family.

Chuang-tzu does none of these things. On the contrary, he sits in a most indecent position, like a wild man or shaman, plays an instrument, and sings happy songs.

7 The reason he gives is yet another reflection on the nature of death: it is merely a phase of change or transformation in the greater course of life, a return to the original state of "undifferentiated chaos" from which we all came. As the Tao-te-ching says:

> What we call Tao is undifferentiated chaos.
> Chaotic! Yet within it are forms.
> Undifferentiated! Yet within it are things.
> Wondrously obscure! Yet within it is ch'i .
> Truly real: it is the perfection of all. (chapter 21)

Why weep if all we do in dying is return home? Why mourn for someone who has just returned to a state that is perfect and from which he was never really separate?

8 This teaching has had a lasting effect in later Taoism, which frowns on wailing and crying in front of a corpse. As described in my *Monastic Life in Medieval Daoism*, the sounds of sadness will tie the leaving souls to the earth and show a massive lack of understanding of the ongoing process of change.

Chuang-tzu's wife died. Hui-tzu (Huizi) went to express his condolences and found him sitting on the ground with legs spread wide, beating a drum, and singing happily.[6]

Hui-tzu was scandalized. "She lived with you, she raised your children, she grew old with you. Now she is dead, and you're not even crying! Instead you beat this drum and sing! Isn't that rather extreme?"

Chuang said, "Not really. Right after her death, I was totally bereft and deeply affected. But then I thought about her beginnings and realized that she hadn't been alive then either. Before she was born, she had no bodily form. Before she had a bodily form, she had not even a breath of vital energy.

"Intermingling in undifferentiated chaos, change happened and there was vital energy. Another change happened and there was bodily form. Then another change occurred and—presto!—there she was: alive. Now there has been yet another change, and she is dead.[7]

"These changes proceed one after the next, just like the four seasons move from spring to fall, from winter to summer. See, now the person lies there, sleeping in the great chamber of the universe. If I went and mourned her by wailing and weeping, I figured I'd just show that I had no understanding of the underlying patterns of destiny. So I stopped."[8]

—CHAPTER 18

9 Continuing to explore how best to relate to death, the Chuang-tzu tells the story of four old men who have realized a more appropriate attitude. They want to be friends with anyone who no longer thinks of his body as a separate, integrated entity but instead feels that it is the same as the universe: head, spine, and buttocks *are* in fact life and death.

10 With an understanding like this, even an extreme disease cannot disturb your inner equilibrium but only gives rise to a sense of marvel and amazement. Just look—what strange changes are happening in the world! Even with his body bent completely out of shape, different outgrowths rising from its parts, and hardly able to breathe anymore, Mr. Car is calm and relaxed.

11 Even more, he is able to see the wonder of it all and speculate what other amazing changes there might be. If part of him became a rooster, he could crow to announce daylight; if another part became a bow, he could shoot his supper; and if he became a horse and chariot, he could ride around.

This rather extreme speculation on the possibilities of bodily change, the interconnectedness of different species and human artifacts, brings home the same point again: all we are is just one aspect of the greater flow of existence, which manifests itself in constant change that is completely beyond our control and about which we can do nothing. Why not make the best of things in the different circumstances and enjoy them for what they are without trying to improve or enhance them?

Four old men called Rite, Car, Plow, and Come were chatting leisurely.

One of them said, "Who can think of one's head as original nonbeing, of one's spine as the process of life, and of one's ass as death? Who really feels that life and death, existing and perishing are just different aspects of one and the same system of change? I would like to be friends with him!"[9]

The four men looked at each other and smiled. None feeling any discord in his heart, they became friends.

Soon after this, Mr. Car got sick and Mr. Rite went to see him. He said, "How great! Look at this process that creates all things! It is making me all twisted!"

He was all crooked and bent over, his spine sticking out, his five limbs pointing in all directions, his chin hidden by his navel. His shoulders were higher than the top of his head, which was crowned by an ulcer pointing to the sky. He gasped to catch and expel his breath, yet his heart-mind was at ease and none of this caused him any concern.[10]

He limped over to see himself in a well. His only comment was, "Oh my! Now the process of creation has really made me crooked and bent over!"

Mr. Rite asked, "Do you resent it?"

"No, why should I resent it? Let's pretend it would change my left arm into a rooster; then I could use it to tell the time of night. Let's assume it made my right arm into a crossbow; then I could use it to shoot an owl for roasting. Let's see: if it changed my butt into a wheel and my spirit into a horse, then I could use them to ride around in. What other vehicle would I need?[11]

(continued on page 41)

12 This is being fully relaxed or letting go completely. It means being at ease with the realization that all the great things on earth—life and death, major gain and loss—come at their own speed and in their own good time. Not letting go, on the other hand, means trying to affect great universal patterns with the small activities and limited impact of a single human life. It creates entanglements, fetters, and bondage to things and people, and ultimately will not affect the patterns of heaven—the natural flow of life at large. The trick, then, is to know which is which—what is part of heaven and what can and do we affect?

13 Heaven—inherent natural flow—is what gives ultimate commands, the word for "command" (*ming*) being the same as that for "fate" or "destiny." Just as children obey their parents in all major decisions and activities, so we should attune ourselves to the will of heaven and learn to simply follow its directions.

Here Chuang-tzu again describes life and death in four stages: obtaining physical form, coming to life, growing old, and dying—in other words, gestation, birth, life, and death. There is nothing we can do about this sequence of human life. Even if we manage to ease one phase or delay the other, they still follow along inexorably and march us along a set path. Since they are all part of the same continuum, it makes no sense to see one as wonderful and another as horrible.

14 If we try to become something we are inherently not, we behave just like the metal in the forge that wants to be a great sword and not an ordinary implement. As the metal has no control over what it is to become, so we as beings on the planet have no control over what inborn qualities we have, what situation we are born into, what chances life will offer, and how many years we are supposed to stay on earth. Dying, then, is part of the preordained course of life and is best seen as going into the blissful sleep of undifferentiated chaos.

"So just think: all gain comes with time; all loss follows its pattern. As long as you relax with the times and settle back into the patterns, there won't be any cause for joy or sorrow. This is what the ancients called letting go completely. But if you can't let go, then things will keep you entangled in all sorts of ways. And since ultimately things can never overcome the powers of the natural flow of heaven, what is there to resent?"[12]

Soon after this, Mr. Come fell ill and was gasping at the point of death.... He said, "Father or mother sending a child in any direction— east, west, south, north—she obeys their command. Yin and yang directing a person—they have more power even than the parents. Now they are bringing me close to death. Should I not listen to their command, I would be obnoxious indeed!

"The Great Clod [of creation] has burdened me with having a body, labored me with coming to life, relaxed me as I grew old, and is now ready to give me rest in death. So, for this reason, when I see my life as a good thing, I should also see my death as a good thing.[13]

"Think of a great smith forging metal. What if the metal were to leap up and say, 'I must be made into a [great sword like] Moye'? The smith would certainly find it highly inauspicious. Similarly, in fashioning a body, what if the cells were to scream, 'We must become human, we must become human'? The process of creation would find that extremely weird.

"Taking heaven and earth as a great furnace and seeing the creative process as a great smith, where would they send us that would not be right? So now I am ready to complete my life in blissful sleep, to eventually wake up again as something else."[14]

—Chapter 6

15 This answers the question of what is heavenly and what is human. Anything pertaining to the flow of life as such—the inevitable unfolding of growth and decline, old age and death—is heavenly and thus predictable and inevitable. Anything that has to do with specific activities, with getting or letting go of certain things or opportunities, is part of the human condition and forms an essential aspect of living in the world. There is, therefore, a set framework of destiny that we cannot change or transcend. But there is also a great deal of room to work within this structure.

16 Thinking of heaven and earth as our father and mother, we should develop an attitude of gratitude and loyalty; we should be willing to give up our lives and livelihoods for them—and even more, letting go of all egotistic pursuits and seeing ourselves as followers of a greater dimension.

17 This is the best way to feel safe and secure: by "hiding the world in the world," by being part of the greatest and most powerful process in the universe. Join heaven and enjoy a sense of oneness and continuous security. Keep to your limited possessions and pursuits, on the other hand, and however hard you try to protect your goods and advance your plans, you never know when someone will come along or something will happen that makes them all come to naught. Knowing that all our activities, however worthwhile, are always subject to influences beyond our reach and ken, we can develop a sense of detachment and inner calm that opens us to the experience of perfect happiness.

Life and death are original destiny; as constant and predictable as the succession of night and day, they depend on heaven. On the other hand, whatever you receive or give up in the course of life is part of your condition as a living being.[15]

People claim to regard heaven as their father and love him with their whole being—how much more should they do for that which is even greater? They claim to see the ruler as superior and to be ready to die for him—how much more should they do to attain perfection?...[16]

Now, you can store your boat in a deep mountain ravine that in turn is hidden in a marsh and think of it as secure. Still, in the middle of the night a strong man may come and carry it off on his back—all the while you are asleep and know nothing about it. So, whether big or small, you can store anything as safely as possible in a suitable place, yet it may get away from you. But if you hide the world in the world, there is no place it could be taken to; this would truly match the encompassing condition of living things.[17]

(continued on page 45)

18 Here is one more funerary custom Chuang-tzu uses as an example of how to change people's attitude toward destiny and death. Rather than requiring fancy coffins, ornaments, and burial goods, he just uses what is already there—demonstrating his oneness with the greater flow of life. The same attitude also appears in a story about the third-century poet Liu Ling as recorded in the fifth-century collection *Shih-shuo hsin-yü* (*Shishuo xinyu*; New Tales of the World):

> On many occasions Liu Ling, under the influence of wine, would be completely free and uninhibited. Sometimes he would take off all his clothes and sit naked in his house.
>
> Once some people came to see him and chided him for this behavior. Liu Ling retorted, "I take heaven and earth for my pillars and roof, and the rooms of my house for my pants and coat. And now, what are you gentlemen doing in my pants?" (chapter 23)

19 Nor does Chuang-tzu worry about what happens to his body; it will feed some animal no matter where it is left, and it is best to be fair to all. One-sidedness in any form only creates more one-sidedness, be it physical imbalance, communal unfairness, or political inequity. To prevent murders by imposing the death penalty, in this thinking, only leads to more killing.

He then implies that his disciples are merely "bright guys" who try to do their best but depend on their senses for information, are entangled in things, and have a limited outlook. He himself, on the other hand, is a spirit person who thinks it all through and sees the bigger picture—the bigger picture where life and death are part of the same continuum and where we are all ultimately one in and with undifferentiated chaos.

When Chuang-tzu was close to death, his disciples wanted to prepare for a sumptuous burial.

Chuang-tzu said, "I take heaven and earth for my inner and outer coffins, the sun and the moon for my jade disks, the stars and constellations for my pearls and beads, and the myriad things for my parting gifts. The furnishings for my funeral are already prepared; what is there to add?"[18]

"But we are afraid the crows and vultures will eat you, Master!"

"Above ground I will be eaten by crows and vultures; below ground I will be eaten by worms and ants. How partisan to take from one group to give to the other!

"If you use imbalance to achieve balance, your balance will be out of kilter. If you use speculation to establish solid thinking, your thinking will be specious. Bright guys are mere servants of things; only spirit people can think it all through. It has always been true that bright guys cannot hold a candle to spirit people—they are fools who rely only on what their senses tell them and immerse themselves in the human realm. All their efforts are wasted—what a shame!"[19]

—CHAPTER 32

1 What, then, is the position of human beings within the greater scheme of the universe? How are we connected to heaven and earth? Why are we what we are? Why do we do what we do?

In the beginning, the world was chaos and nothingness. There were no beings; they could not be named. Out of chaos, the first stage of pre-creation forms, a state of universal oneness. This is still undifferentiated, but it is no longer completely formless. It carries the seed of division into yin and yang and thus of the creation of all things.

2 As things are created, they continue their connection to this underlying creative oneness, which is described in terms of "inherent potency" or "virtue" (*te/de*). The term expresses the manifest activity of Tao, the spiritual potential and inherent power of things, the sense of inner truth that is individual yet also formless. Receiving the particular share or "allotment" of Tao and inherent potential determines each being's station in life and developmental potential. This is original destiny, the command every one of us gets from the universe to come to life in this particular shape and situation.

3 Birth in an individual body, then, occurs when these various potencies take physical shape, when they receive ordered structure or principle. This further determines our particular essential nature, our unique character and abilities, the patterns we use as we live in the world.

4 Finding this true pattern, realizing our essential nature, we can recover the connection to inherent power, to the level of original oneness. This is a state of cosmic harmony within, the full realization of destiny, the recovery of cosmic oneness, the merging with the great flow of Tao.

4 □ Cosmos and Destiny

In the cosmic phase of Grand Initiation, there was nothingness: nonexistent and nameless. From here oneness arose: existent yet without distinct forms.[1]

Things attained this oneness and came to life—we speak of their inherent potency [virtue]. They still were without distinct individual form, but they each had their allotment [from Tao] and remained close to it—we speak of their original destiny.[2]

With continued unfolding, things came forth. As things were completed, they gave rise to ordered structure [principle]—we speak of their form. Their physical form contains spirit, each with its peculiar manifestation—we speak of essential nature.[3]

When essential nature is cultivated, it returns to potency; when this is perfect, you are at one with Cosmic Initiation. At one, you are empty; empty, you are great.

It is like closing the beak and silencing the singing [of a bird]. Closing and silencing produce a state of harmony of heaven and earth. This harmony made permanent, you are as if ignorant, as if immersed [in Tao]—we speak of mysterious potency. It means being at one with the Great Flow.[4]

—CHAPTER 12

5 Destiny is the fundamental connection we have to life, the basic social place we are born in, the inherent pattern of our most basic relationships. Duty, on the other hand—a term also translated as "righteousness" or "social responsibility"—describes our relation to community, social institutions, state, and world. Neither destiny nor duty can be escaped; by birth in a certain place and with certain abilities and characteristics, we are tied into the structures of kinship and society.

Doing our best to serve these and not having much choice most of the time, we do whatever is necessary as things arise. This is how we fulfill our destiny and complete our duty.

6 Yet, at the same time, we also have our heart, which connects us to inherent power, the level of our being that is part of heaven and earth. We follow that while going along with the demands of duty and destiny, never letting emotions or frustration deter us from who we are and what we do best.

Serving the family and the world, you can forget what Chuang-tzu calls the "social self." The word *shen*, also a term for "body," is the socially established self as opposed to *hsing*, the physical form (rendered "body"). The social self involves having emotions and frustrations and striving for things beyond original destiny or inherent power. Throughout Taoist history, cultivation in many forms has served to eliminate this constructed self in favor of the pure body, the recovery of essential nature, and the fulfillment of destiny.

7 To sum up, relax and just go along with things, understanding that there is a lot you cannot change, yet always find things to nourish the inherent potency that is part of your cosmic being. This is what fulfilling destiny means—not a deterministic position of helplessness but the effort to be what you truly are and to do what you do best without trying to change yourself or the world.

Confucius said:

There are two great containing forces in the world: destiny and duty. The love of a child for the parents is destiny; it can never be extirpated from the heart. The obedience of a citizen to his country is duty; wherever you go there is always government and you cannot get away from it anywhere between heaven and earth. These are the great containing forces.

Thus in serving the parents, you do not choose the place or time but just do it—this is filial piety at its utmost. In serving the country, you do not pick the specific matter or situation but just do it: this is patriotism at its fullest.[5]

Similarly, in following your heart, you don't allow mere emotions of sadness or joy to change your course; you know that you cannot change things and just do it—this is inherent power at its utmost.[6]

Being a child and a citizen, you often have no choice. Acting in perfect service in any given circumstances, you completely forget the social self—how could you still have time to relish life or hate death?...

It is best to relax your heart-mind and just go along with things. Comply with what you cannot change and nourish your inner core— this is perfect! Why would you try to recompense anyone or make up for failures? There is nothing better than to fulfill your original destiny— but, boy, is it ever hard to do![7]

—CHAPTER 4

8 "Capacity" translates *ts'ai* (*cai*), a word usually associated with things like talent, inherent ability, and natural skill. In this context, it is another term for essential nature and original destiny, the forces that make us unique and tie us to the Tao.

9 To maintain and fulfill our true capacity, it is essential to realize that there are quite a few things in life we have no control over—they are the workings of destiny, the things we are fated to encounter and commanded to experience by the inherent patterns of heaven and earth. It is futile to speculate about why or how they come about; it is meaningless to try and understand their workings—they are there, and that is it.

On the other hand, it is essential to keep calm about these experiences. Letting go of tensions, giving up trying to change things we have no control over, we can relax with who we are and where we are in life. In this way the mind is balanced, the heart is joyful, and we can connect with the underlying potency of life at all times.

10 Remaining calm and in mental balance, restful within and cool without, we continue to connect to the underlying level of cosmic oneness, to the inherent potency of Tao. This is always present yet also always formless—it cannot be lost, only clouded. Being connected to it, we reach internal harmony and can see and feel what is right in any given moment, where our original destiny ends and the demands of the constructed self begin.

Duke Ai, talking to Confucius, asked, "What does it mean to say that my capacity is fulfilled?"[8]

"Life and death, existing and perishing, success and failure, wealth and poverty, worthiness and low status, praise and blame, hunger and thirst, heat and cold—all these change over time and are the workings of original destiny. They come and go before us like day and night, and we can never understand their cause or beginning.

"Therefore, these things should be no reason to disturb your inner harmony and should never enter your heart. Make sure you remain calm and at peace, going along with all and never subject to joy or hate. Make sure you remain on an even keel day and night and join all things in their spring. Thereby you stay connected with life in your heart at all times: this is what we mean by saying that 'capacity is fulfilled.'"[9]

The Duke asked next, "What does it mean to say my inherent potency is formless?"

"Balance is best seen in the complete stillness of water. Use this for your model: on the inside contained, on the outside unruffled. As for inherent potency, its cultivation allows you to reach internal harmony. Inherent potency being formless means that things can never lose it."[10]

—CHAPTER 5

11 Here is a concrete example of what the examination of destiny means. Sang is so poor that his friend worries about him after a week of rain and takes him something to eat. Sang himself wonders why he has come to this condition and tries to find someone to blame. But there is no one. It is just the workings of fate.

The same sequence is later taken up in one of the key texts on Taoist meditation, the *Tso-wang-lun* (*Zuowang lun*; Discourse on Sitting in Oblivion) by Ssu-ma Ch'eng-chen (Sima Chengzhen; 647–735), a major ritual master and patriarch of the school of Highest Clarity. He says:

> Heaven and earth are equable and regular, protecting and supporting all without personal aims. So if I am poor now, it is certainly not the fault of heaven and earth. When parents give birth to a child, they desire to see him in wealth and high esteem. So if I am poor now, I cannot blame it on my parents. Other men, ghosts, and spirits don't even have the time to save themselves; how then would they have the strength to make me poor? Going back and forth, I cannot find anyone to blame for my poverty. Thus I cannot help but realize that it must be my own karma, my own heaven-given destiny. (section 5)

He not only adds the section on ghosts and spirits being too busy to worry about a single individual, but also connects the concept of original destiny to the idea of karma—the Buddhist notion of cause and effect in human life. Introduced into China in the early centuries CE, it has been part of Chinese culture ever since. It states that all actions have inevitable consequences and, after a period of maturation, revert to their perpetrator not only in this life but—transmitted through soul, spirit, or consciousness flow—in innumerable rebirths as well.

As do the early texts, so later Taoists insist that the remedy lies in giving up trying to understand or change things and instead working to connect to the deeper levels of cosmic harmony.

Yü and Sang were friends. Once it rained continuously for ten days, and Yü was worried that his friend might be in trouble. So he wrapped up some food and went to give it to him.

When he reached his door, he heard strange sounds—singing and crying, drums and guitars, and some words: "Is it my father? Is it my mother? Is it heaven? Is it the people?"

It sounded as if Sang could hardly bear it, the words were just rushing from his mouth.

Yü went in. "What weird song is that?"

"I was thinking," Sang explained, "what it was that brought me to this extreme poverty, but I couldn't figure it out. Is it that my father or mother wished me to be so poor? Is it that heaven, which covers all impartially, and earth, which sustains all equally, would concern themselves with me personally and take the trouble to make me poor? I was trying to find out who did this to me and couldn't find an answer. Still, here I am—dirt poor! It is destiny!"[11]

—Chapter 6

12 Connecting to a deeper harmony, however, does not necessarily mean eschewing the pleasures of life. Thus, the sage ruler Yao—a major Confucian culture hero and the epitome of filial piety and social responsibility, who should know all about duty and destiny—is shown to actively reject all the good wishes for long life, wealth, and children. His reason is that they cause nothing but worry, trouble, and embarrassment. He prefers to live a non-life in order to stay safe and hates to venture out into the world and engage himself fully out of pervasive anxiety that things may go awry.

13 Yao is quite wrong, of course. Destiny means engaging in life as it comes along and leaving things we cannot change to the powers that be. Plus, in the Taoist vision, the universe is a positive force, and there is the firm conviction that unless there is a place for anyone or anything, heaven would not bring it forth to begin with. So, having children means that somewhere there is a place for them, having material wealth means that somehow we can do some good with it, and having a long life means that the world can make use of our talents and abilities. There is no need to actively eliminate any of them.

14 Still, there is a way of being in the world that is more restful than others: living unobtrusively, consuming little, and not imposing our way or wishes on others; enjoying life when things go well in society, withdrawing and resting when there is nothing much to participate in; living to realize our potential but without imposing it on others; engaging in what is most meaningful to us without grasping for more than our proper share.

15 Having reached that, we are never far from the connection with cosmic potency. Eventually we return to the purer levels of Tao and ascend to the immortals—beings of pure spirit who reside in paradises, galaxies of subtle energies that are closer to the creative center than this world. The classical image is of the successful immortal being received in a cloudy chariot and ascending in triumph, having lived a life of spiritual purity and free from all harm.

The sage ruler Yao came to inspect the border point at Mount Hua, when the customs officer addressed him: "Oh, a sage has come! May you be blessed! May you have a long and fruitful life!"

Yao said, "No, thank you."

"May you be rich!" "No, thank you."

"May you have many children!" "No, thank you."

"Long life, wealth, and many children are what all people want. Why don't you?"

"Many children mean lots of worries, wealth means lots of troubles, and long life means lots of opportunities for embarrassment. None of these three nurture inherent potency, therefore: No, thank you."[12]

"Wow. First I thought you were a real sage, but now I see you are just a public figure. When heaven brings forth the myriad people, it provides roles for all of them. So, if you have many children and they all have their place in life, what is there to worry about? Similarly, if you have great wealth and share it with others, what trouble would you have?[13]

"Now, a real sage lives unobtrusively like a quail and consumes little like a hatchling; he moves about freely like a bird, neither leaving traces nor trying to change things around. When the world is in line with cosmic order [Tao], he shares in the prosperity of all. When the world is in disorder, he cultivates his inherent potency and pursues his leisure.[14]

"After a thousand years, he gets tired of all this and leaves to ascend to the immortals. Riding in a chariot of white clouds, he reaches the realm of the gods. Afflictions of any kind never get close to him, and he is always free from misfortune—what embarrassments might he face?"[15]

Yao, stunned, proceeded to ask, "May I ..."

"No. Just get away with you!"

—CHAPTER 12

16 This sums it all up: get a feeling of where you are in life and don't worry about what you are not; get a sense of where your destiny is taking you, what your best abilities are, and what fulfills you the most, and don't concern yourself with whatever is not part of this.

17 While destiny will take care of a lot, you can't just sit back and do nothing. You need to nurture your body and make it comfortable—but don't overdo it, since any excess will cause harm. And, yes, take good care of yourself so you stay alive as long as you can—but when life is gone, don't try to prolong it artificially.

18 There are some people who think they are their bodies and just working out and taking supplements is enough to keep themselves alive. But life is so much more. Yes, it is good to be fit and strong and healthy, but a vibrant spirit, an open heart, joy in life, and a sense of cosmic connection go far beyond staying in good shape.

Good-shape practices are what the Chinese call techniques of "nourishing life" (yang-sheng), methods that form part of preventive medicine and serve to keep us young and vigorous well into old age. They include breathing exercises, physical workouts, dietary suggestions, sexual hygiene, and meditation, but fundamentally all center around moderation and finding what is right for ourselves.

Since we are alive in a body, we cannot help but try to stay healthy and find the best daily rhythm, the most nourishing food, the ideal form of exercise, and the most comfortable and best-looking clothes. We may not really want to do this, but it is part of being human and thus forms yet another aspect of original destiny. This, too, connects the individual to Tao.

Connecting to the essential workings of life, you do not labor over what life cannot do. Connecting to the essential workings of destiny, you do not labor over what knowledge cannot figure out.[16]

To nurture your body, you must first support it with all sorts of material things, but it may also happen that you have too much stuff, which then prevents you from taking proper care of it.

To nurture your life, you must first make sure it does not leave the body, but it may also happen that people keep your body functioning when there is really no more life to speak of.[17]

When life comes, you cannot make it go away; when it leaves, you cannot keep it. Too bad! Ordinary people think that nurturing the physical body is enough to preserve life. But when nurturing the body is not enough to preserve life, then what would be sufficient?

Yet, even though we may realize that all the little things we do to keep our bodies going are ultimately not enough, we cannot keep ourselves from doing them anyway. These actions are part of life and we cannot avoid them.[18]

—CHAPTER 19

Body and Mind

1 The self is a complex issue, and the Chinese have a variety of terms and concepts relating to it. Here the first understanding is of the self as body—but what is this body? The Chinese view the body as an integrated system of energy centers (inner organs), ch'i channels (meridians, blood vessels, bones), and connections to the outside world (orifices, acupuncture points).

Chuang-tzu here lists the hundred bones or joints, major skeletal mainstays, with the number "hundred" meaning "many"; the nine orifices, which are the two eyes, two ears, two nostrils, and the mouth, plus anus and urethra; and the six inner organs—heart, spleen, stomach, lungs, liver, and kidneys.

2 The parts listed are over a hundred, and there are many more. Which of them, then, is the "self"? Which is most important? Which is the real chief? The upshot is that they all work together, but there is no stable, discernible pattern, and we really have no idea who and what we are. Just like the universe, the body is a functioning organism over which we have no control.

3 The body throughout all its life inexorably runs toward death, and however hard we work, whatever we do makes no difference. The fundamental human condition, then, is quite dreadful and pitiable—an inherent lack of constancy and real knowing.

4 This sense of complete confusion about who we are, although frustrating, is yet a good thing. It is the starting point for a new and different vision of the self and the world, the beginning of critical reflection and a step back from simply running after things. The same is also expressed in the Tao-te-ching:

> I alone am inert, showing no sign, like an infant who has
>   not yet smiled.
> Forlorn like one without a home to return to.
> I have the mind of an idiot, so chaotic and dull!
> Ordinary people are bright and intelligent—I alone am
>   chaotically dull!
> Ordinary people are farsighted—I alone am blindly chaotic!
> (chapter 20)

5 □ The Self

The hundred bones, the nine orifices, the six inner organs[1]—they come together and exist here as "me," yet which of them should I think of as really being myself—or should I enjoy them all equally? Is there one that is more personally "me"—or are they all just there to serve, like associates and concubines? Is their combined service sufficient to maintain order? Do they take turns as master and servant, or is there a real chief among them? I keep searching for answers, yet whether I find some actual pattern or not neither enhances nor diminishes the system's inherent perfection.[2]

Once we receive this complex physical form, we never forget its functions as we move inexorably toward the end. Whether in conflict with things or in alignment, we run toward the end like a galloping horse that no one can stop. Isn't it pitiful?

All our life we keep on laboring hard and never see any lasting results. We are utterly drained from all the labor and never know where we will eventually go. Isn't it dreadful?[3]

Some say, "But we're not dead yet!" What good is that? Our body changes without stopping and our mind goes with it. Isn't it deplorable? Is human life really such a mess? Or am I the only one messed up and all the others are really okay?[4]

—CHAPTER 2

5   Nan-jung Chu is a fictional seeker in the Chuang-tzu. Lao-tzu is the ancient thinker who served as an archivist at the royal court in Lo-yang (Luoyang), the capital of Chou, and was known as a very learned man whom many people consulted. A rather legendary personage, he is also the alleged author of the Tao-te-ching.

6   Ch'u is the southernmost of the ancient states, in the area south of the Yangtze. Lao-tzu's place is in Lo-yang on the Yellow River. The distance is considerable, and even today it takes some time to get there.

7   Lao-tzu here refers to the many different voices we carry around in our heads. Just as the body consists of all the different parts and we don't know which one is the real "me," so the mind has multiple aspects and desires that pull us in different directions. Modern psychology calls them subpersonalities and, as shown in Debbie Ford's *The Dark Side of the Light Chasers*, has developed visualization techniques to flush them out and create a balance among them.

8   Different social demands, then, such as knowledge and ethical behavior, put the individual in a quandary: either we are socially in trouble or we cause harm to ourselves. This self, moreover, is divided into the personal, social, and object self. They are all socially constructed, purposefully envisioned versions of who we are—as personalities, in society, and in relation to the material world. They all require different sets of subpersonalities to create a semblance of functioning, yet none of them is truly "me."

9   Look for your true essential nature and a way of life right for yourself. Thus Lao-tzu continues to advise Nan-jung to meditate and focus within, to learn when to stop pretending, engaging, and consuming. Become like an infant; act without thinking—just be.

Nan-jung Chu (Nanrong Zhu) took some supplies and traveled for a week without stopping until he reached Lao-tzu's place.**5**

"Hi," he said, "have you just come all the way from Ch'u?"**6**

"Yes, indeed."

"And why did you bring this big crowd of people along?"

Startled, Nan-jung turned to look behind him.**7**

"You don't have a clue what I mean, do you?"

Nan-jung hung his head in shame, then looked up and sighed. "Just now I forgot how to answer—I just lost this 'me.'"

"What does *that* mean?"

"If I don't know anything, people call me a total idiot; but if I know things, they come back to haunt my personal self. If I am unkind, I harm others; but if I practice kindness, it comes back to haunt my social self. If I neglect my duties, I cause injury to others; but if I fulfill them, they come back to haunt my object self. How can I ever escape? These three trouble me a lot. So I came all the way from Ch'u to ask your advice."**8**

Lao-tzu said, "Looking you right in the eye, I got a good sense of who you are, and your words just now confirm it. You appear confused and frightened as if you had just lost your father and mother and are trying to find them with a long pole at the bottom of the sea. You have lost your true way of being human—you are completely lost and disoriented. You want to get back to your true essential nature and find the way of life that is right for you, but you have no clue where to start. Pitiful, indeed!"**9**

—Chapter 23

10 The Tung-t'ing Lake is a flood basin for the Yangtze in northeast Hunan. Hsien-ch'ih is the name of an entrancing kind of music.

11 The point here is that whatever we consider our self is stimulated and modified depending on outside sensory input. Our emotions and reactions are not constant; here they are described in terms of fright, relaxation, and confusion. Modern psychology, especially as represented in the work of author and psychologist Daniel Goleman, divides emotions into withdrawal and approach reactions, leading to patterns of behavior that either reject or seek out material objects, personal relationships, or body sensations.

12 Chuang-tzu connects the different reactions to various levels of being: human, heavenly, energetic, and cosmic. The human level is one of constant anxiety and insecurity; the heavenly is peaceful and flowing; the energetic level finds stability in ethics and a positive outlook; the cosmic—symbolized by the sphere of Great Clarity, a major Taoist heaven—is marked by confusion, the state of being "chaotic and dull," which is closest to original creation.

13 Universal naturalness or spontaneity (*tzu-jan/ziran*) means matching your actions and feelings to both your inner truth and the current state of outer affairs without getting entangled or upset. Its practical application is nonaction, a way of living in the world that is not passive but also not intrusive or coercing. The five virtues are later called the five phases—developmental stages in the continuous unfolding of yin and yang, from rising yang (spring, wood) through the height of yang (summer, fire), a balance of yin and yang (late summer, earth), and rising yin (fall, metal) to the height of yin (winter, water).

14 Music is a great metaphor for the energetic patterns of the universe; both work in multiple combinations that can be in harmony or dissonance. This connects Taoist thinking to physics, both the law of resonance and wave theory, and also to the quantum world, both working with subtle vibrations, waves and energies that come together in a variety of ways.

Northgate Cheng said to the Yellow Emperor, "Your Majesty was playing Hsien-ch'ih (Xianchi) music in the wilds around Lake Tung-t'ing (Dongting).[10] When I first heard it, I was frightened. Then I listened some more and found I was getting languid. As I listened to the last part, I was totally confused—bewildered, speechless, like I couldn't get hold of myself."[11]

"That's quite normal. I played it with human means, attuned it to heaven, executed it in accordance with propriety and righteousness, and elevated it to the level of Great Clarity.[12]

"To create perfect music, first match it to human affairs, then let it follow the principles of heaven; execute it in accordance with the five virtues, and match it to universal naturalness.[13] Doing so, it will be in balance with the four seasons and find great harmony with the myriad things; it flows just like the seasons arise one after the other, and all things come to life in their turn. Rising and falling, the civil and military strains each take their turn; clear and turbid, yin and yang notes move in harmony.[14] The sounds like floating light, hibernating insects start to move; an awesome spectacle, thunder and lightning arise....

"This music first made you frightened: that's a state of awe. After that, I moved on and you felt languid—that's a state of flow. In the end you were confused—that's a state of innocence. Innocence is close to Tao—you can hold on to that and take it with you."

—CHAPTER 14

15 Although we tend to have specific reactions—of withdrawal or approach—to outside stimuli, there is no inherent need for them. We don't really have to have feelings that end up creating tensions and desires. We can rest instead in inner constancy and just be.

16 Spirit and essence are two major forms of *ch'i* in the body. Spirit is the subtler, faster-vibrating level of vital energy, the force that makes up the psychological, intellectual, and spiritual dimension of the person. Essence is its thicker and more tangible form, which consolidates in bones, hair, nails, and the brain and which is most importantly manifest in reproductive fluids, such as sperm and menstrual blood (believed to coagulate inward to form the embryo). Externalizing the spirit means giving up psychological integrity for outside goals; burdening the essence means wasting precious fluids for nonproductive purposes.

17 Things like "hard" and "white" are topics the Logicians worried about: "a white horse is not a horse." They indicate being involved in extraneous and ultimately irrelevant issues to the detriment of inner integrity and energetic wholeness. Emotions and feelings, to sum up, are nonessential and distracting; they do not add to your basic station or purpose in life but harm the various aspects of *ch'i*.

Hui-tzu asked Chuang-tzu, "Can a person really be without feelings?"

"Of course."

"A person without feelings, how can you call him human?"

"Tao gave him visible appearance, heaven gave him bodily form— why not call him human?"

"But—if you call him human, how can he be without feelings?"

"This is not what I mean when I speak of feelings. What I mean when I say he is without feelings is that the person does not allow likes and dislikes to enter and burden his social self, but always goes along with his inherent naturalness, never trying to improve on life."[15]

"Without improving on life, how can he even have a social self?"

"Tao gave him visible appearance, heaven gave him bodily form, and he does not allow likes and dislikes to enter and burden his social self. You, on the other hand, externalize your spirit and burden your essence,[16] you lean against a tree and moan, hang over your desk and go to sleep. Heaven gave you a human body and you mumble about dialectics like 'hard' and 'white.'"[17]

—CHAPTER 5

18 While it is good not to have strong emotions or attachments to any kind of constructed "self," it is even better to take complete control over your energy and learn to manage different ways of appearing to the world without losing your inner core. This story contrasts a shaman with a master of Tao. Shamans in traditional China were trance experts who could communicate with the gods, either by ecstatically traveling to them or by inviting possession, to foretell the future, heal the sick, change the weather, and so on. They were technicians who used a variety of instruments (such as the diviner's compass and various charts) and interpreted cosmic patterns (such as the stars or bodily signs). They were not, however, close to the root of creation or striving for cosmic oneness.

19 This passage provides a rare glimpse of the competition among masters in China (then as much as now) and the—always essential— requirement to fully commit to one single spiritual teacher to fully realize his way.

20 Like the music story above, this tale divides patterns according to earth, heaven, essential energy, and creation. Earth is like wet ashes, dark and without movement. The "core" or central moving point of inherent potency (virtue) is closed and latent, like earth in winter—a force to be reckoned with but not visible or tangible.

There was a shaman in K'ang (Kang) called Chi-hsien (Jixian). He knew all about people's life and death, existing and perishing, good fortune and disaster, longevity and early death, foretelling all by year, month, week, and day as if he were a god. Locals thought him a warlock and crossed the street when they saw him coming.[18]

Lieh-tzu (Liezi), however, was fascinated by him and told his teacher, the Gourd Master, about him: "Originally I thought your teaching [Tao] was great, but now I am not so sure. This guy seems to be even better."

"So far, I have taught you the basic framework of my teaching. I haven't really gotten to the meaty parts yet. But you think you've got it all. Even with a host of hens, if you lack a rooster, how will you ever get eggs? Similarly, when you give a teaching to the world, you can spread it around, but there must be sincere faith.[19] Then you can get to a point where you can make people see different patterns in your looks. Try to bring your shaman over and I'll show you."

The next day Lieh-tzu came with the shaman to see the Gourd Master. Upon leaving, the shaman said, "I'm so sorry! Your master is a dead man. He won't even live to the end of next week. I saw something strange about him. He looked like wet ashes."

Lieh-tzu went back in and wept until his shirt was soaked with tears, then told the Gourd Master.

He responded, "Just now I showed him the pattern of earth. Things were sprouting but without dynamics or regularity. So what he saw was the core of my inherent potency all closed up.[20] Try bringing him again."

(continued on page 71)

21 The state of heaven is a sense of complete flow, a way of being with multiple options and innumerable variations, a sense of fluidity and openness—like the ink blots in a Rorschach test that can be seen and experienced in any number of ways. Energetically it means a sense of being alive and radiant.

22 The *Lieh-tzu* (*Liezi*; Book of Master Lieh), another early Taoist text that was lost and later reassembled, adds the nine names. They describe the different aspects of the perfect mind using the character for "water," as opposed to words with "heart," which describe emotions and attachments (which people should do without):

> Whirlpools, still waters, currents, water bubbling up from the ground, water dripping from above, water slanting from the side, water dammed and turned back, water draining away in a marsh, several streams coming from one source, and the all hollowed-out deep pool. (chapter 2)

Each of these stands for a particular state of the primordial mind, which is at the same time pure mystical spirit—from the water that has not yet emerged from the source, through the vastness of the primeval ocean, the beginning stages of heaven and earth that are without name or substance but already working, to the pattern of earth, which is "still and silent, nothing moving, nothing standing up." In addition, water can also represent the more ordinary activities of the mind, then described as running, gurgling, springing, whirling movement, and its reactions to the senses, which are duly expressed as confusion, muddle, turbidity, and excitement.

The power of pure energetic flow is its very instability, its constant change—the shaman has no way of pinning it down, but the master can modify and experience it as needed.

The following day, Lieh-tzu brought the shaman again. After seeing the Gourd Master, he said, "Good thing your master met me! He is on the mend and again full of life! I saw his condition stabilized."

Lieh-tzu reported.

The master said, "This time I showed him the appearance of heaven. Name and reality were not fixed, but core energy was rising up from my heels. So what he saw was the core of basic wellness.[21] See if he will come again."

The next day, Lieh-tzu came once more with the man to see the master. Upon leaving, he was exasperated. "Your master is never the same! I cannot understand his appearance. Have him steady himself, and I will see him again."

Lieh-tzu told the Gourd Master.

"Right now," he explained, "I showed him the pattern of cosmic dynamics that none can overcome. So what he saw was the core of my vital energy in perfect balance. Where swirling waves come together, there is a deep pool; where still waters come together, there is a deep pool; where flowing waters come together, there is a deep pool. The deep pool [of the perfect mind] has nine names and I have shown him three.[22] Try bringing him again."

(continued on page 73)

23 This, finally, is the human mind before creation: pure emptiness, inherent openness—a vague, indistinct, chaotic, humming sense of being that has no form, no character, no time, no space. It just is, and we are constantly part of it. It is the core of our inherent potential, the aspect of our inner being that connects us to the deeper levels of the universe, the Tao within.

It is too much for ordinary people and completely overwhelms the hapless shaman. But it is the only dimension where we can find something even vaguely akin to some true self, a sense of being at home in the cosmos, a feeling of oneness with all.

The following day, Lieh-tzu again brought him to see the Gourd Master. However, before he had even sat down to examine him, the shaman lost his composure and ran away.

"Run after him," the master shouted.

Lieh-tzu ran in pursuit but failed to catch him. He came back, panting, "He's gone. He's off. I couldn't catch him."

"This time I showed him the pattern of not-yet-beginning, before I even came to be. So what he saw was pure emptiness, writhing snakelike, not knowing who or what, at times not even there, at times flowing in waves. That's why he fled."[23]

—CHAPTER 7

1 This famous "butterfly dream" continues the theme of the self, not so much in terms of the different parts of the body and the requirements of society, but in terms of personal perception and the sense of certainty of who we are. The self, it turns out, is undefined, fluid, in transformation, a nonentity, nothing we can firmly pin down.

Chuang-tzu uses dreams and dreaming variously as a way of illustrating this fluidity of self-identity. They serve as an expression of loosening the ties to what and who we believe we are. There is ultimately no way of knowing whether we are in fact who we think we are or whether we are—as some religions have claimed—lost souls in search of our true home that have erroneously, precipitously, or for some more or less obscure reason been caught in this particular body and on this particular planet.

The butterfly, of course, is a symbol of that true inner part in many cultures. It is also a spontaneously recurring image in the dying, especially in dying children. It stands for the sense of complete freedom and release, the power of inherent transformation, the opening of ourselves to new realms, new visions, and a different dimension of reality.

6 □ Dreams

Once Chuang Chou dreamt he was a butterfly, flitting and fluttering about as butterflies do. He had a wonderful sense of pleasure and felt greatly alive. He had no idea that he was Chou.

Suddenly he woke up and could clearly sense that he was Chou.

But then he did not know whether he was Chou who had just dreamed that he was a butterfly or whether he was in reality a butterfly who was now dreaming that it was Chou.

Still, Chou and the butterfly have to be somehow separate—or do they? This is what we call the changes things undergo.[1]

—CHAPTER 2

2 Proper mourning behavior demands that a person wail and cry, wear sackcloth and ashes, show deep distress, and grieve heartily for all to see. Meng-sun Chai here does all these things to good outward show, yet his mind is free.

This is yet another expression of the fluidity of self, manifest in a division between the conscious creation of a certain self-image and the actual feelings we have within, between the demand of certain social situations—which require that we look and behave in a specific manner—and the way we would really like to be. Here the self is an outward performance, a vision that is mainly in the eye of the beholder.

Yet, there is also the reverse of this, which comes into play in religious formalities and the practice of Tai Chi Chüan (taiji quan) and Ch'i-kung (qigong): the more we physically embody certain attitudes, the more we adapt them as the way we are—the "fake it till you make it" or "smile and you will feel better" of modern self-help culture. Here the self is learned and malleable; we can make ourselves into whatever we choose—or can we?

3 The best attitude for Chuang-tzu is one of "unknowing," accepting the different changes and transformations without trying to understand, evaluate, or influence them. From this position of an inner sense of change into which you can relax with ease, your outer appearance becomes just a formality, necessary to hold society together but without impact on your true being—which rests in the greater universe and flows along with life and death as a fluid pattern. Again, the image of the dream makes this attitude easier—how do we know that we know?

Yen Hui asked Confucius, "When Meng-sun Chai's (Zhai) mother died, he wailed without shedding tears, his heart was free from distress, and he managed the funeral without sorrow. Although he did not express himself in tears, distress, or sorrow, people thought him a top mourner in the state of Lu. Is it really possible to get famous for something without any trace of reality behind it?[2] I find this very weird."

Confucius replied, "Meng-sun did all he had to and was known for that. He tried to simplify the whole process and did not quite manage to, but he did simplify it somewhat.

"Meng-sun does not know what causes life or what makes people die. He has no clue what comes first, no idea what comes next. He happened to undergo a change and become a living being, so now he waits for he-does-not-know-what to change him yet again. Then, once he gets close to that change, how does he know he hasn't changed already? Once he is in a place with no change, how does he know that was a change earlier? Just like you and me: isn't it possible that we are in a dream from which we have not yet woken up?[3]

(*continued on page 79*)

4 Another part of this sense of fluidity is the division into body and mind, the physical husk and the spirit. The Chinese do not make the radical distinction of body and soul Western and Indian cultures make; to them, they are different aspects of one universal and ubiquitous vital energy that yet vibrate at different frequencies and speeds.

Still, subjectively there is a difference: the body is a fragile, physical form; the mind-and-heart (the same word, *hsin* [*xin*], in Chinese) is a psychological entity that has thoughts and emotions. Similarly the person physically is strictly temporary, subject to disease and decline, while the spirit is free from all, a cosmic part within people that represents the freedom of Tao on earth. Being closer to the spirit within allows a sense of wider openness, the freedom from all dying and decay.

5 Not just a butterfly—in our dreams we can be all sorts of things: birds, fish, and even creatures that do not usually exist in the world. Yet what is ultimately real? Who are we in essence? Which of the different identities we take on in life and sleep is permanent, solid, a firm ground for understanding, evaluating, making decisions? For the Chuang-tzu, none of them. We do not ultimately know.

6 However, this is no reason to despair. You can enjoy encountering something delightful in the course of life; you can also "keep smiling" when things are difficult with an attitude that accepts the fluidity of existence and identity. Even better, you can find an inner sense of composure, of relaxation into the various changes, and from this central hub or core let yourself go along with all. This, then, is how you reach a sense of flow, of being with the current of life and Tao, of finding oneness with heaven—the natural pattern of existence.

"Also, he may be a fragile physical form but there is no loss in his mind-heart; he may be a temporary hut [of the spirit], but there is no sense of death in him.[4] Meng-sun is really awake: when others cry, so does he, but from his own motivation and perspective.

"Now, we all speak of ourselves as 'I,' but how do we know what that really is? You may dream you are a bird and fly across the sky, that you are a fish and delve into deep waters. If you think of it—we don't really know, do we? Which of these is being awake? Which of these is dreaming?[5]

"Encountering delight is not as good as smiling no matter what; smiling at all times is not as good as being fundamentally composed. Being composed deep within and letting oneself go along with the various changes—this is how you get to flow in oneness with heaven."[6]

—CHAPTER 6

7 Here is a concrete case of someone suffering an apparently terrible fate that then turns out to be a good thing. It is a lesson for all situations. We do not know what is happening or why. Things may look bleak but turn out very well; things may seem great but result in difficulties. We simply don't know—so there is little point in racking our brains and making evaluations and decisions. Life is and remains unpredictable, and even death may turn out to be a great party after all.

8 Dreams in some cases compensate for what we don't have in life. The Taoist text *Lieh-tzu* has several stories where people make up in their dreams for what they don't have in life—the rich man who labors all night long in captivity, the impoverished waif who feasts at wonderful banquets. They each wake up to a completely different reality, but in their minds they taste the other side and so have a more balanced life.

In modern understanding, too, dreams serve a compensatory function, helping us come to terms with information received during the day, assisting the brain to clear its channels for new things. In some cases, people also have lucid dreams, where they control their contents and manage the direction they take. Later Taoists engage in active dream practice, setting certain goals and patterns for the mind.

9 The more we can control the dreaming process, the more we realize that there is nothing we can take for granted. We may think we are awake, that things and people are a certain way, yet ultimately none of that is real, permanent, or reliable. Even our own "waking" identity is nothing but a dream, and we meet other dream entities in a process that is also nothing but a dream. Even the idea that sometime down the line a great man will come to explain it all is ludicrous—the wondrous and fabulous are just as dreamlike as the daily and familiar.

How do I know that loving life is not a delusion? How do I know that hating death is not like having lost your way and not knowing the way home? Lady Li was the daughter of the border guard of Ai. When the Duke of Chin (Jin) first took her captive, she cried till her dress was soaked. But after she reached his palace, shared his luxurious bed, and ate his delicious meats, she felt sorry for her tears. Along the same lines, how do I know that the dead do not feel sorry for their former craving for life?[7]

You dream of enjoying a fun party and wake up crying the next morning. You dream of crying sorry tears and wake up to go off hunting. While you dream, you have no idea that you are dreaming—you may even be trying to interpret your dream while you are dreaming. It is only after you have woken up that you know it was actually a dream.[8]

In the same way, there may well be a great awakening, after which we shall know that life is actually a great dream. Yet so many people remain ignorant, thinking that they are awake, brightly insisting that they know what is what, assuming one is a leader, the other a servant—how thick is that!

Confucius as much as yourself—you are nothing but a dream! And when I say that you are a dream—well, that in itself is a dream also. These very words of mine should really be called pure fantasy! After ten thousand generations we may encounter a great sage who knows how to explain everything—and this, too, may be as commonplace as seeing him every morning and evening.[9]

—CHAPTER 2

10 This brings up the question of how we can communicate at all, how we can ever know what someone else might feel. The greatest divide is across species: the fish in the river seem to be happy, swimming about and flitting to and fro. But how do we know that our idea of "happiness" applies to them at all? Don't we just create an image of "happiness" and see it reflected in the movements of the fish?

Hui-tzu makes this very clear, but Chuang-tzu takes it one step further: even within our own species, we cannot really know what someone else is thinking, what their experience is like, what they know. We can only try to communicate with very limited means and vaguely approximate what we know and feel.

11 The other part of it is, though, that we can just be where and how we are. Living clearly in the present moment and staying connected to being present provides spontaneous insight. There is a way to be in perfect happiness and at one with the cosmos—found by letting go of conscious evaluations and pretensions, language structures and thinking patterns, by learning to just be.

Chuang-tzu and Hui-tzu were taking a walk crossing the bridge over the Hao River and looking into the water. Chuang-tzu said, "Look at all these little fish, how they flit about and play! This is the happiness of fish."

"You are not a fish," Hui-tzu countered. "So how do you know the happiness of fish?"

"You are not I. How do you know that I do not know the happiness of fish?"[10]

"I am not you and I certainly do not know what you know. But just as certainly you are not a fish and you do not know the happiness of fish. So, there!"

"Let us get to the root of this now. You said to me, 'How do you know the happiness of fish?' At that point you already implicitly knew that I knew it—and that's how come you asked the question in the first place. And indeed, I know it just by being here on the bridge over the Hao."[11]

—CHAPTER 17

12 This story is a classic on the theme of reality. Reality is one thing; how we see it and react to it is another. In fact, we do not react to the way things are, to any actual reality, but to our feelings about it. Reality in itself is completely subjective.

Think of music—you may really like hard rock or rap, which to your parents is just noise. Or of sights—you may totally detest a certain outfit or pair of shoes, which to the wearer is the height of fashion. Smells, tastes, touch—they are all like this, which is why we have a perfume and soap industry, cuisines from all different countries, various kinds of fabrics, body lotions, and so on.

13 The trick, according to the Chuang-tzu, is to let go of right and wrong, good and bad, likes and dislikes, to learn to accept that reality means different things to different people. It is best to stay calm and relaxed, centered and focused, resting in "heavenly balance." But why is it so difficult to do that?

Once a monkey keeper was getting ready to feed acorns to his charges. He said, "I will give you three in the morning and four in the evening."

The whole tribe was furious.

"All right," he said, "I will give you four in the morning and three in the evening."

They were all highly delighted.

The reality behind the words was no different, yet they evoked great anger and joy in his charges. And this is typical.[12]

The sage, on the other hand, lets right and wrong be as they please and rests in heavenly balance. To him, all goes.[13]

—CHAPTER 2

1 The key to understanding the human predicament and the main pivot of change is the mind. What, then, is the mind?

The answer to this question has many levels. On a cosmic level, the mind is the working energy of spirit within us, the force that dwells in our physical form and animates it, the fundamental factor that makes people and animals be alive. The mind is thus an individualized and personalized—and often distorted and alienated—form of the spirit, which in turn is the universal, cosmic energy of aliveness.

It is intangible and yet very much present. The little piglets in the story notice that it is gone when their mother is no longer alive. It is the soul energy that people feel leave when they are present at someone's death—the factor that is highly disputed in cases of coma or brain death: what is it that determines "life," and when can it be said to no longer be there?

2 Further metaphors illustrate the concept. Someone who has lost a foot, due to amputation or injury, no longer needs shoes. A soldier who died in battle in ancient China is believed to have moved on to the otherworld speedily; he thus has no need for the feathery ornaments that serve the soul in its transition. In either case the idea is the same: there is no physical basis for the need any longer.

7 □ The Human Mind

Confucius said, "I once was sent to go to Ch'u and on the way I saw piglets trying to feed off their dead mother. After a little while, they looked startled and all ran away. They no longer saw themselves in her; they no longer felt they were part of the same species. They loved their mother, all right, but what they loved about her was not her physical form but that which animated this form.[1]

"When a soldier dies in combat, his folk do not bury him with feather ornaments; when someone has lost a foot, he couldn't care less about shoes—in all these cases the foundation is gone."[2]

—CHAPTER 5

3 This story describes the situation of a man getting river water for his vegetables. He carries one pitcher after another, which is highly laborious and quite inefficient. Tzu-kung, one of the disciples of Confucius, happens along and offers him a machine to do the job—using little effort and gaining high efficiency.

The mind here is the inventor of devices. It examines a situation critically and comes up with ways of dealing with it in a different way, usually asking how we can make our lives easier. At the same time, while we do this, we sacrifice the connection to our labor and our personal involvement. Some meditation traditions try to reverse this; Thich Nhat Hanh, in *The Miracle of Mindfulness*, speaks ardently of the benefits of doing the dishes by hand, being fully present in the action, feeling the water, the soap, the brush, and having a direct relationship to the things we use.

4 Chuang-tzu calls the mind that seeks efficiency at the cost of direct connection the "mechanical mind." It is a detached way of relating to things in the environment that sees the world (and the body) in terms of a machine and its parts, that exploits nature, things, and other people—instead of relating to their inherent potency, to the spirit in everything.

Modern psychologists, such as Arthur Deikman in *The Observing Self*, call it the "object self"—a way of seeing everything around us (and eventually also ourselves) as mere objects to control, manage, and replace as needed.

5 This objectified, mechanical way of relating to the self and the world constitutes the loss of Tao. Tao manifests in spirit, the inherent potency of aliveness, and as such is always present as long as we live. But to activate it we must maintain an inner purity, an innocence, a spontaneous and indeed spirited relationship to existence. The mind, then, in its tendency to objectify and mechanize that relationship is harmful, an aberration.

Much better to let it go and develop a state of "no-mind," a key term also in Zen Buddhism, where it indicates something quite like Nhat Hanh's "mindfulness": a way of being fully present.

Tzu-kung (Zigong) had been traveling around Ch'u [in the south]. On his way back to Chin (Jin) [in the central plains], he passed the area north of the Han River and saw an old man working in his vegetable plot. He had dug an irrigation ditch to bring [river] water to his well and was now carrying it pitcher by pitcher to pour over his plants. He was working hard, expending a great deal of effort with minimal visible results.

Tzu-kung watched him for a while and then said, "You know, there is an apparatus for this. In one day it can water a hundred fields. It requires minimal effort and brings great visible results. Wouldn't you like one like that?"

The gardener looked up at him and asked, "How does it work?"

"Well, it's a mechanical device made of wood that is heavy at one end and light at the other. It lifts the water as with a ladle, almost as if it was bubbling over. It is called a well-sweep."[3]

The gardener turned red with anger, then laughed derisively. "I have heard about this. My teacher used to say that having a mechanical apparatus, you inevitably do things the mechanical way, and before you know it you have a mechanical mind.[4]

"Once you carry a mechanical mind in your chest, your internal purity, your innocence, is no longer complete. Once your innocence is gone, your spirit and life are no longer stable. Once you live with instability, the Tao no longer has a place to rest.[5] It is not that I don't know about mechanisms like this—I just won't use them!"

—CHAPTER 12

6 Another aspect of the mind—which underlies its ability to analyze things and come up with mechanical devices—is its tendency to use language: terms and classifications. It needs this to stay oriented in the world and thus gives names to everything. The question here is: can we use the term "Tao" to refer to existence as a whole?

7 The answer is really "no," because Tao is simply too big for language of any sort. On the other hand, the question is the starting point for an examination of the analytical mind and its linguistic conventions, which create the reality we live in. Ten thousand is a big number and becomes the signifier for "a lot," which should really be "innumerable." Heaven and earth are the two main supporters of life on the planet; they are the name used for the universe, which is not just big but immeasurable.

Yin and yang indicate the basic energetic patterns of the world, rising and sinking, expanding and contracting, moving and resting, and so on; they, too, are incomprehensible. They are also at the core of the fundamental Chinese pattern of analysis, which was correlative thinking, unlike in the West, where the world is seen through linear analysis that focuses on logic and the law of cause and effect.

In either system, the mind recognizes and classifies similarities and differences between structures and understands reality in terms of a particular dynamic of interaction among the different aspects. In a next step, the analytical pattern creates a specific vision of reality, a paradigm into which all experiences fit, and new realities are formed on the basis of further association. The analytical mind is thus the slanted, pre-patterned mirror through which we see reality. It is another function that separates us from Tao.

Knowing Little asked, "So if we just speak of Tao in reference to existing things, will that do?"[6]

Great Balance replied, "Oh, no! Let's just think about counting all the many things on the planet—there is no way they stop at ten thousand, yet we call them the 'ten thousand things' just to signify that there are a whole lot. In the same way, we speak of heaven and earth when we try to talk about the greatest of physical forms; we speak of yin and yang when we try to point to the most fundamental of vital energies. Tao—that's a different story; it's everywhere. We can use the term because it is so great, but what could we ever compare it to?[7] Arguing like this is like comparing dogs with horses—how can it not be totally off the mark?"

(continued on page 93)

[8] The four directions are the cardinal directions of east, west, north, and south. The six harmonies are the energies of the four directions plus up and down. The question asks how best to understand the patterns of existence.

[9] The two main dynamic tendencies in the universe are yin and yang; the most basic pattern of time is the four seasons. Between them they bring forth a continuous flow of rise and decline, up and down, and so on, which in turn leads to the differentiation of the sexes, human emotional reactions to reality, feelings of security and bad luck, as well as different forms of behavior. The entire gamut of human life patterns is thus predicated on the underlying patterns of the cosmos.

[10] The mind likes to analyze and describe, deliberate and categorize. It creates order and systems, lays out principles and developmental paths. It continues to classify and give names to reality, when words and knowledge cannot in fact reach it.

From the perspective of Tao, there is no point in all this activity. It just creates a vision of reality, a mere smoke screen of apparent knowledge, that can never really touch the whole in its full complexity. Better to stop right here.

Knowing Little continued, "How, then, within the four directions and six harmonies, do the ten thousand things arise?"**8**

Great Balance said, "Yin and yang radiate upon each other, cover each other, regulate each other. The four seasons succeed one another, producing and destroying each other in turn.

"From this, desire and hatred, pursuit and withdrawal arise; male and female, joining and separating begin. Security and peril follow each other; good and bad fortune give rise to one another. Leisure and haste take their turn; assembly and dispersal come and go.**9**

"All these things can be designated in name and reality; they can be recorded in their essentials and fine points. They follow an order that matches certain principles; they proceed along a course that can be guided. They move in patterns: rise and recede, end and begin—over and over. This is how things exist: where words stop and knowledge ends. They are ultimately just things and nothing else.

"Seeing with the Tao, don't pursue them to where they perish nor seek them out where they arise—stop examining right here."**10**

—Chapter 25

11 This passage introduces yet another form of mind: the sensory mind of desires and emotions. It enjoys or "relishes"—and thus craves—certain things that make it feel good: basic delights of vision and hearing, more advanced joys of virtuous behavior (including the four main Confucian virtues), and various intellectual kicks, such as trying to develop wisdom and knowledge.

However, these each create problems of their own: sensory indulgence, a separation from inherent potency and cosmic principle, as well as different forms of unnatural, artificial, and contrived behavior. This type of mind, its mechanical and analytical forms, thus puts up yet another barrier to connecting with Tao, to living fully in the world, and to being who we really are.

12 The alternative is to "rest in your core," to know who you are and allow the various senses and their experiences to just come and go. This is the way to be. But most people don't know who they are, and the various aspects of the world and sensory patterns pull them in every which way, so that great disorder results. We don't just do what we feel is right for us at a deep level. Seduced by the sensory mind, we listen to what others say, follow what advertisers want us to be, obtain what the market wants us to buy—continually defining our self through outer aspects.

13 In addition, all these sensory desires are formalized in certain behavior patterns and ritualized in social conventions—described here in terms of the classical patterns of Chinese religious rites. Participants fast for a few days, abstaining from sexual and sensory involvement, before they chant the scriptures; they kneel in formal garb during the actual ceremony, the presentation of prayers and offerings; and they join the community in celebrating the rite with music, song, and dance.

All these activities, which are of course also activated through the body and thus made to feel "natural" and "necessary," just serve to reinforce a conceptualization of reality that is really just that—a conceptualization.

Do you relish clear vision? You just indulge in colors.

Do you relish keen hearing? You just indulge in sounds.

Do you relish benevolence? You just spoil inherent potency.

Do you relish righteousness? You just oppose cosmic principle.

Do you relish propriety? You just encourage artificiality.

Do you relish music? You just encourage lascivious tunes.

Do you relish sageliness? You just encourage artistry.

Do you relish knowledge? You just encourage fussiness.[11]

As long as people in the world rest peacefully in the core of their essential nature and original destiny, these eight may be around or not—who cares?

But the moment people don't rest peacefully in their core, these eight cause decay and distortion and bring disorder to the world. As soon as people start to respect and care for them, there is great delusion everywhere![12]

And do you think they just do this once and then let them go? Oh, no. They celebrate them with all kinds of ritual: fast before they speak of them, kneel before they present them, and drum and sing before they dance to them![13] What, then, are we to do?

(continued on page 97)

14 The text encourages us to be like the "superior person," the gentleman (*chün-tzu/junzi*) of the Confucians who adopts an attitude of "nonaction" (*wu-wei*).

This does not mean doing nothing, becoming like a vegetable, or being totally spontaneous without any planning whatsoever. Rather, it means letting go of egotistic concerns and desires on the personal level, finding a sense of where life, nature, and the world are headed on the social level, and abstaining from forceful interference in the political realm. The Tao-te-ching says:

> *Act on things and you will ruin them.*
> *Grasp for things and you will lose them.*
> *Therefore the sage acts with nonaction and has no ruin,*
> *Lets go of grasping and has no loss.* (chapter 64)

15 Relaxing in nonaction, you can feel calm and contented, with the five inner organs—the repositories of vital energy in the body and also the seats of the emotions (heart—joy, lungs—sadness, spleen—worry, liver—anger, and kidneys—fear)—at peace and the senses (also matched with the organs) free from distraction. Then pure spirit starts to shine forth, and you can be completely still and rest in utmost silence. This in turn has an impact on your senses; they become much sharper and more powerful as and when the mind gets out of the way.

If you get to be like this, you'd be the kind of person we'd want in government—a person with a great sense of inner centeredness, who values his or her own truth more than fame and fortune, who can allow all things and beings to go their own way and do their own thing. Such a leader really has no interest in analyzing or managing anything!

Well, ideally we should be like the superior person who gets involved in managing the world yet finds the best attitude to adopt is nonaction. Relaxing into nonaction, he or she can rest peacefully in the core of essential nature and original destiny.[14]

The person who values his or her self more than governing the world—that's the one you can actually trust to run the world.

The person who loves his or her self more than governing the world—that's the one you can actually give the world to manage.

A superior person who can keep his or her five inner organs free of turmoil, his or her vision and hearing free of disturbance—that's the one who will sit still like a corpse and have vision like a dragon, will be silent like a deep pool and have a voice like thunder. The spirit of such a person moves, and the world follows! Such a person relaxes in nonaction, and the ten thousand things come to obey! "I have no time to govern!"—that's his motto.[15]

—CHAPTER 11

16 Someone like this has a "complete mind," a mind that is whole in itself, rests in nonaction, and responds to things in spontaneous flow. This is the mind to make our "teacher," the guiding light in all activities of daily life. Plus, it is not far to seek; everybody has it. It is just that people don't use it—instead of working with the mind that is inherently complete and thus just a function of spirit, they partition it into sections and separate it from life, creating classifications and categories that are ultimately absurd.

17 But it is also possible to use the various kinds of mind that we have been equipped with. However, after use, you have to let go, just as you would get rid of a fish trap or a rabbit snare. Similarly, language and all mental classifications and evaluations serve a certain purpose—to convey your situation and position in life—but once you get the idea, you can let them go. Getting away from speaking and categorizing is the way to get closer to heaven. As the Chuang-tzu says in chapter 32:

> To know Tao is easy, but not to speak about it is hard.
> To know and not to speak—this is reaching heaven.
> To know and to speak—this is staying with humanity.
> The perfected goes for heaven, not humanity.

If everybody just followed their complete mind and made it their teacher, then who would be without a teacher? Why must you know and classify and arrange things instead of letting the mind take it all in spontaneously? Even idiots have this mind. Living with a mind that is not complete and classifying things according to right and wrong— well, that's like saying you are going to Yüeh (Yue) today and arrived there yesterday![16]

—Chapter 2

A fish trap is used to catch fish; get your fish and forget the trap.

A snare is used to catch a rabbit; get your rabbit and forget the snare.

Words are used to convey ideas; get the idea and forget the words.[17]

Oh, how I would love to talk with one who has forgotten all words!

—Chapter 26

Self-
Transformation

1 Hsü Wu-kuei is a lesser Taoist master whose teachings are included in the later chapters of the Chuang-tzu. The art of evaluating animals and people by their looks is called physiognomy. It is a classical form of fortune-telling in China and works by looking at facial features, bone structure, and patterns of movement.

2 The three types listed here represent the dominant ways of being in the world: the most common is determined by sensory desires and their immediate gratification; the second represents the more intellectual and artistic endeavors in human life, with a tendency to look at farther horizons and into the distance; the highest—which is reached by meditation—is spiritual unfolding, a state of oblivion of the self and others where the spirit can shine forth unhindered from the mind.

The Chinese also express these three in terms of psychological agents: the "material soul," which represents our instinctual side and is responsible for survival and sensory satisfaction; the "spirit soul," which is the artistic and intellectual dimension of people and guides us to be altruistic and culturally active; and the "spirit," which is the pure potency of aliveness and connects us to the divine.

3 Inherent qualities are the practical manifestation of inherent potency in the individual, our inborn abilities or natural skills, what we know or can do without active learning or trying very hard.

Being "complete" means that we use these inborn skills without any concern for sensory gratification, conscious aims, or intellectual goals. Going along with the spirit within, we are also highly competent. Subjectively this feels like a loss of identity, oblivion, unknowing, or no-mind. This is where we get closer to perfect happiness.

8 □ Oblivion

Hsü Wu-kuei (Xu Wugui) said:

Let me tell you how I evaluate dogs by their looks:[1]

Those of the lowest quality rush for their food, fill up, and stop: they are showing the inherent potency of a wildcat.

Those of medium quality seem to be staring into the distance.

Those of the highest quality are as if oblivious of who or what they are.[2]

But the way I evaluate dogs is nowhere near the way I examine horses. They gallop in four ways: straight as if following a plumb line, curved as if following a curve, square as if following a carpenter's square, and circular as if following a compass. All these are fit for a kingdom but can't hold a candle to those fit for the empire.

Empire-level horses—their inherent qualities are complete. They are as if anxious, as if forlorn, as if they had lost their identity. Horses like these go faster than any, rushing along and spurning the dust. They simply don't know where they are.[3]

—Chapter 24

4 The far north in Chinese cosmology of the five phases or five elements is associated with water, winter, the color black, and darkness. It is the direction where the sun is hidden before it again rises in the east and is thus the area of highest potential, of greatest mystery. There, true wisdom can be found; however, it is beyond language and expression.

5 Tao in this passage means "flow of life," the sense of being "in the flow" or "in the zone," a state of happiness within the self and perfect functioning within the world. We all want that, and we'd love to have conscious, clearly outlined, and practical techniques to get there. We want concrete information, preferably a detailed path. We'd like to see clear methods that can be appreciated with our senses, evaluated and discussed intellectually, and adopted in a course of systematic practice.

6 However, these clear methods are hard to come by. The three figures Knowledge meets on his quest represent three levels of relating to Tao: the stage of complete unknowing, knowing and being oblivious, and knowing and putting into words. The last one represents the common human mind.

Meditation practice reverses the journey and leads to the first stage. It is defined as the inward focus of attention in a state of mind where ego-related concerns and critical evaluations are suspended in favor of perceiving a deeper, subtler, and possibly divine flow of consciousness. A method of communicating with hidden layers of the mind, it allows the subconscious to surface in memories, images, and thoughts while also influencing it with quietude, openness, and specific suggestions.

7 So, if there is any guidance at all on the problem of how to get to be in the flow, it is to let go and be free—on all levels: thinking, living, and practice. The main tenet of Taoist meditation is accordingly to let go, release, diminish, and forget.

Knowledge went hiking in the far north and reached the area of the dark waters, where he climbed the hill of Hidden Heights.[4] There he encountered No-Action No-Speech and said:

"I would like to ask you something. How do I arrange my thinking, what conscious organization do I need to understand Tao? How do I adjust my lifestyle, what practices should I follow to be at ease in Tao? What prerequisites are there, what methods do I follow to fully attain Tao?"[5]

He asked these three questions, but No-Action No-Speech made no answer. It was not that he made no answer; he did not know *how* to answer.

Knowledge, not receiving any information on his questions, returned south to the region of the bright waters, where he climbed to the top of Lonely Pass. There he saw Crazy Crooked and asked him the same questions.

Crazy Crooked replied, "Ah! I know. I will tell you." Just as he wanted to speak, however, he had already forgotten what he wanted to say.

Knowledge, still not receiving any answers, returned to the imperial palace. There he had an audience with the Yellow Emperor and once more asked the same questions.[6]

The Yellow Emperor replied, "To let go of all thinking and be free from conscious organization is the first step toward understanding Tao. To let go of all lifestyle concerns and be free from any sense of practice is the first step toward being at ease in Tao. To let go of all prerequisites and be free from any systematic path is the first step toward fully attaining Tao."[7]

—Chapter 22

8 Fasting (*chai/zhai*) means to purify oneself in preparation for a ritual. It involves abstention from meat and the so-called "strong vegetables," which include garlic and different kinds of onions. It also includes celibacy and distance from pollution (dirt, blood) as well as some positive measures, such as bathing in fragrant water, wearing freshly laundered clothes, and letting go of worldly concerns.

The word *chai* over time expanded in meaning and came to indicate vegetarian meals—rather than fast, it came to be a purified form of feast. Among monastic Taoists in the Middle Ages, it duly indicated the ceremonial meal taken at noon. Another meaning of the term was "temporary renunciation." It meant that laypeople could join the monastic community for a few days at a time, taking extensive precepts and living in purity to renew themselves.

9 Fasting is also a common metaphor for meditation, then seen as a mental diet of concentration on one object or detached observation (mindfulness). The more the practitioner rests the mind, the more it releases compulsive thoughts, pent-up tensions, and suppressed emotions. It has been found very effective in stress reduction and the strengthening of positive emotions.

The practice outlined here describes moving away from processing reality through the senses and instead using the mind as the primary function of perception, then going on to working with pure *ch'i*, or vital energy. Both the senses and the mind are cluttered, restricted by artificiality, and tend to hold on to things. *Ch'i*, on the contrary, is fluid and open—empty of emotional reactions and preconceptions.

How do we perceive reality with *ch'i*? By not evaluating but merely receiving, feeling subtle energetic vibrations, and allowing intuition to take over—by letting go of the self and others.

Yen Hui said, "This is as much as I can do by myself. May I ask how to proceed from here?"

Confucius replied, "Fast! I will tell you. Do it with full intention—it's not easy, to be sure. If you take it easy, bright heaven will not support you."

"My family is poor. We often have no wine or rich foods for months together. Is this what you mean by fasting?"

"This is the fasting you do before a sacrifice. It is not the fasting of the mind."**8**

"Please, what is this 'fasting of the mind'?"

"Unify your will and don't listen with your ears, but listen with your mind. No, don't listen with your mind, but listen with your ch'i. Listening stops with the ears, the mind stops with perception, but ch'i is empty and waits on all things. Tao gathers in emptiness alone. Emptiness is the fasting of the mind."**9**

(continued on page 109)

10 Reaching this state of "emptiness," you can move about in the world but should remain without active pursuits or desires. You can and should do what is needed, but not hang about when things are done. Rather than striving for success and recognition, you should find a way to rest completely in the way you are naturally without thinking or trying to do or attain anything.

11 The image of walking about and leaving traces stands for the way of being in the world—all the different activities you undertake. The moment you are in the world, you are bound to have an impact, to leave a footprint. It is not too hard to move about and be careful, to do things and try to minimize the changes you bring to the planet. It is much harder to never even touch the ground, to live as an embodied being in the world and yet float above it.

By the same token, it is easy to fake competence and status and admirable qualities with people, to pretend to be someone fancy, to match or exceed social expectations and plant a glowing image of yourself in the minds of others. But you can't do that with heaven, the aspect of nature within and the greater cosmic context. The goal is to get to the heavenly and thus closer to perfect happiness with no pretense.

12 Like everything else, this heaven-based lifestyle needs a root in the person: our inherent potential and inherent qualities. We need this to live our best life as much as a bird needs wings to fly, as the brain needs information to understand.

13 In many meditation traditions a bright light is a common sign of internal opening, when thoughts have subsided and emotions have calmed down. On the other hand, when we try to sit in meditation and are assaulted by innumerable thoughts of what best to do and how to find good opportunities, we don't actually meditate but "sit and run around." Eyes and ears focus inward; one detaches from body and mind and listens to the voice of heaven within. From here, the mind can radiate outward, and pure spirit and aspects of divinity come to dwell.

"Before I received your instructions, I was thinking of myself in concrete terms. After I learned this method, I am no longer there as an entity. Is this what you mean by 'emptiness'?"

"Indeed. Let me tell you. You can enter and move about in the world, but don't be concerned with fame. If invited, go and do your part; if not, just stop. Be without any obvious openings and without any poisonous feelings about the world. Just rest in yourself completely without the need to attain anything—that gets you pretty close.[10]

"Not leaving any traces is easy; never even touching the ground is hard. Dealing with people, faking it is easy; dealing with heaven, it is very hard.[11]

"I have heard that beings with wings can fly; I have never heard of creatures without wings doing so. I have heard of people understanding things on the basis of information; I have never heard of anyone understanding things without it.[12]

"Sit quietly and look at your inner space—an empty room that brings forth a bright light. There all thoughts of good luck and fortune stop. If they don't stop, we call it 'sitting and running around.' So, let your ears and eyes focus inward and your mind's knowledge radiate on the outside. Then divine entities will want to be part of you—how much more will human beings be attracted?"[13]

—CHAPTER 4

14 This classic passage on how to proceed to a state of complete oblivion again uses a three-part system. First, you eliminate "benevolence and righteousness," classic Confucian virtues that stand for ways of behavior in the world, the need to submit to social conventions, the desire to win approval in the world.

15 Next, you give up "rites and music," which indicate a sense of propriety and a feeling for rhythm and social patterns. They stand for internalized behavior patterns, a personal conscience, and inner monitoring—the little voice that says, "You really should do this" or "Better stay away from that."

16 Eventually you can let go of all, give up physical and intellectual identity, and become one with "Great Pervasion," the great thoroughfare of Tao. Sitting in oblivion here is both an advanced state of meditative absorption and a way of being in the world that is free from reflection and intentional action, a spontaneous way of living in natural simplicity realized by being at one with Tao.

Over the centuries, "sitting in oblivion" has also come to denote a distinct method of meditation, a way of physically taking a certain posture and working with the mind. As such it is still practiced in Taoist monasteries today. As described in my *Sitting in Oblivion*, in the Tang dynasty (618–907), the expression stood for an integrated system of practice, a seven-step process that also includes methods of concentration, mindfulness, and ecstatic journeys as well as prescriptions on diet and breathing—formulating just the kind of conscious lifestyle directives that Chuang-tzu insists we should forget all about.

Yen Hui said, "I'm getting there!"

Confucius asked, "How so?"

"I am oblivious about benevolence and righteousness."[14]

"That's great. But not quite it."

The next day he was back again. "I'm getting there!"

"How so?"

"I am oblivious about rites and music."[15]

"That's great. But not quite it."

The next day he was back again. "I'm getting there!"

"How so?"

"I can sit in oblivion!"

Confucius was startled: "What do you mean, 'sit in oblivion'?"

"I let my limbs and physical structure fall away, do away with perception and intellect, separate myself from body-form, and let go of all knowledge, thus joining Great Pervasion. This is what I mean by 'sitting in oblivion.'"[16]

"Joined with Tao, you have no more likes within. Transformed in Tao, you have no more guidelines without. You have indeed become a worthy man! May I ask to become your follower?"

—CHAPTER 6

17 This passage gives a more concrete sense of what Chuang-tzu means by oblivion. It is a state where we are naturally at home in the greater universe, as comfortable in our mind and spirit as we are in well-worn shoes or clothes that fit well.

18 Since the match is perfect, there is no need to evaluate it or develop feelings about anything. Since we are the only way we could be as determined by Tao through inherent potential and qualities—as well as essential nature and original destiny—there is no urgency to change or develop regrets about not changing.

19 The ultimate state is being oblivious even of being oblivious, to forget the forgetting. In the early Tang dynasty, Taoists called this "double forgetting." Practitioners must first discard all mental constructs of reality, illusory imaginations based on sensory and emotional evaluations that they project outward to create something they then see as real. Next they must eliminate the underlying activity of the mind, the inherent function of active consciousness that makes sensory perception possible. "Forgetting" both means the reorganization of ordinary consciousness to absolute consciousness and again from absolute consciousness to no consciousness at all in complete oblivion.

20 Another description of the same state from the same chapter likens the mind of complete oblivion to being intoxicated to a point where we do not know what is happening any longer and thus cannot possibly be afraid of anything. This creates a state where body and person stay whole because we no longer react with panic and do all the wrong things.

One is oblivious of the feet when the shoes fit just right; one is oblivious of the waist when the belt fits perfectly.[17]

Knowledge is oblivious of right and wrong when the mind is in perfect alignment with all. No more changing within, no more mere following without—this is how you create perfect alignment with all affairs and events.[18]

Once you reach this level of alignment and you stay in it always, this is the alignment of being oblivious of even the idea of alignment.[19]

—CHAPTER 19

If a drunken man falls off a carriage, he may get hurt but he won't die. He has the same bones and joints as everyone else, but his injury is different because his spirit is whole. He never knew he was riding; he never knew he fell. Life and death, alarm and terror never enter his breast, so he meets peril with no fear. He is like this under the influence of liquor—how much more so under the influence of heaven? Thus as the sage rests with heaven, nothing and no one can agitate him.[20]

—CHAPTER 19

21 The distinction of *ts'ai* and *tao*—inherent qualities and way—is the difference between ability and opportunity. You may have lots of ability to do certain things in life, but the right time and place and chance may never come. Or there may be great possibilities for action in a variety of ways, but you may not have the necessary skills, funds, or connections to do anything. That's where cooperation comes in; one has the skills, the other the connections.

22 This outlines meditative progress in seven stages, which can be divided into three main levels:

1. No more world—no more things—no more life

2. Clarity of dawn—seeing your aloneness

3. Beyond time—beyond existence

The practitioner, as in "sitting in oblivion," puts all ideas of the world, all perception of others (objects and people), and all concerns for his own life outside—letting them go and eliminating them from his mind.

Then he finds an inner clarity or radiance, possibly like the bright light within that signals the opening to pure consciousness, and "sees his aloneness," a state of nonduality that, according to the commentator Kuo Hsiang, means "letting go of whatever one comes in contact with, before or after."

From here, the adept moves on to go beyond time and all existence, reaching to the underlying Tao, the pure power of creation.

23 The Tao, then, never dies and never arises; it is beyond the transformations that characterize life and death. Yet it is also present everywhere, underlying all existence as it passes through alternating states of advance and retreat, growth and decline, movement and rest.

Master Sunflower of South Wall asked, "Can I learn the Tao?"

Woman Hunchback replied, "No! No, you can't! You are not the person for it. Once there was Pu-liang I (Buliang Yi) who had the inherent qualities of a sage but not the way, while I had the way of the sage but not the inherent qualities.[21] So I decided to teach him to find out if he could indeed become a full sage. I thought it would be easy to teach the way of the sage to someone who already had the inherent qualities. So I gave him precise instructions and supported his progress.

"Within three days, he was able to externalize the world.

"Once he could do this, I continued my support, and after seven days he was able to externalize all things.

"Once he could do this, I continued my support, and after nine days he was able to externalize life itself.

"Once he could do this, he went on to achieve the clarity of dawn.

"From here, he went on to seeing his aloneness.

"Next, he went to a state beyond past and present.

"Reaching even beyond, he entered a state where there is neither life nor death.[22]

"What kills life can never die; what creates life can never be born. Once active in the world, it initiates and receives, destroys and creates all there is. Its name is 'Push and Peace.' What we mean by that is that it first gives things a push, then lets them be complete."[23]

—CHAPTER 6

24 Making this Tao your true home is the goal of the practice: taking care of yourself and keeping the senses and mental classifications under control, you will find a state of heavenly harmony, an inner sense of contentment, and divine entities will come to protect you.

The latter are called "ghosts and spirits" in the text; this refers to ancestral spirits and various local and celestial deities that form an integral part of the world in ancient China. They will be attracted to this kind of person, who is fully at one with inherent potential and relaxes in the greater universe. In other words, you are not only free from worry and fear and will stay physically whole, but also the greater cosmos will come to support you.

25 This describes the meditative trance, the deep absorption in nothingness; there is no more identity in either body or mind. The body is like a mere skeleton—in some cases, also described as a "withered tree"—the mind is like cold ashes in the fireplace with no spark of anything. The phrase is also echoed in later Zen Buddhism, which speaks of "body and mind falling away."

26 Another Chuang-tzu phrase that is picked up in Zen is "no-mind," the state of inner perfection, completion, or wholeness that is free from seeking, from any need for outside confirmation. It relates to reality like a pure mirror, perception becoming mere reflection without evaluation or reaction.

As the text says in chapter 7, "The perfect person uses the mind like a mirror: initiating nothing, receiving nothing, responding to things but not holding on to them. Thus he can control them and not be exhausted."

Open Lack asked Covered in Clothes about the Tao. The latter replied, "Take care of your body and unify your vision—heavenly harmony will come to you. Contain your knowledge and unify your conduct—divine entities will want to be part of you. Inherent potency will be your beauty; Tao will be your home. You gaze about like a newborn calf, never trying to find out why."[24]

Before he even finished his words, Open Lack had already gone to sleep. Covered in Clothes found this highly delightful and left, breaking into a song:

> *Body like dried bones,*
>
> *Mind like dead ashes—*[25]
>
> *Perfect in reality and perception,*
>
> *He never looks for reasons.*
>
> *Dim and dark, dark and dim,*
>
> *No-mind complete: can't plan anything with him.*[26]
>
> *What kind of person is that?*

—Chapter 22

1 What, then, exactly is this Tao? This first selection describes it in its cosmic dimension as being beyond life and death, time and space. It comes—we don't know whence; it has no origin as it emerges and is present in the world. It goes—we don't know where; it has no place through which it passes as it leaves the world. Fully real, it cannot be defined in human terms; it has no limits or definition in terms of space and time.

2 Beyond the senses and our intellect, we cannot grasp it in any ordinary way; this is why it presents an opening to heaven, a connecting point of human life to the greater cosmos, a link to both preexistence and post-life. Taoists call the time before creation—both personal and universal—"prior to heaven" and refer to the post-creation world as "after heaven." "Heaven" here stands for the known and experienced universe, and the Tao is the key factor, the connecting pivot that makes it real.

3 Since whatever is cannot be the source of all existence, Tao as part of cosmic beginning is also nonbeing, nothingness, nonexistence—the state underlying all reality and the source of the myriad beings. This state of cosmic chaos, of primordial energy, of original suchness is where the sage or perfected—the person who has realized Tao and resides in oblivion—makes his or her home.

9 □ Realizing Tao

It emerges without origin; it passes without opening. It is real but without firm location; it is extensive but without clear measure. Emerging yet without clear opening, it is real.

Being real but without a firm location refers to space. Being extensive but without a clear measure refers to time.[1]

It lives and dies, emerges and passes, yet one cannot see its form. This is why we call it the gate to heaven. As such it is nonbeing—the myriad things emerge from it.[2]

Being cannot create being; it must come from a state before, which is nonbeing. It is in oneness with nonbeing that the sage finds his home.[3]

—CHAPTER 23

4 Here we have some more concrete characteristics of Tao. It can be eminent and simple, vastly expansive and minutely concentrated. It is like the spirit, which the Tang text *Nei-kuan-ching* (*Neiguan jing*) on "inner observation" describes:

> Spirit is neither red nor yellow, neither big nor small, neither short nor long, neither crooked nor straight, neither soft nor hard, neither thick nor thin, neither round nor square. It goes on changing and transforming without measure, merges with yin and yang, greatly encompasses heaven and earth, subtly enters the tiniest blade of grass.

The list of negatives is similar to those found in other mystical traditions, which too can only list what the divine is not. Thus the Upanishads in India say about Brahman:

> It is not coarse, not fine, not short, not long, not glowing like fire, not adhesive like water, not bright, not dark, not airy, not spacious, not sticky, not tangible. It cannot be seen nor heard, not smelled nor tasted. It is without voice and wind, without energy and breath, without measure and number, without inside and outside.

5 The two main figures here represent the main perspectives on Tao: one remains in a state of unknowing, not even trying to use worldly terms or interpretations; the other provides specific characteristics. Both have it right to a certain degree, but while one of them is completely immersed in Tao, the other is partially separated.

The main distinction made is between inside and outside, a wide-ranging differentiation in the tradition. Inside means esoteric, secret, connected, at one—a state of nondual perception as well as, in a community setting, being part of the inner circle of disciples, ritual, or activities. Outside means exoteric, public, open, separate—a state of mental duality, verbalization, differentiation, analysis, as well as, in the religious organization, being part of the audience, the observers of the ritual, the civil society.

Great Clarity asked Limitless, "Do you understand Tao?"

"No, I don't."

He then asked Nonaction, who said, "Yes, I understand Tao."

"In your understanding of Tao, does it have clear characteristics?"

"Yes, it does."

"What are these characteristics, then?"

"In my understanding, Tao can be noble and humble, connected and scattered. These are the characteristics by which I understand Tao."[4]

Great Clarity reported these words to Nonbeginning. "So this is what I got: Limitless said he had no idea, and Nonaction claimed he understood. Who was right and who was wrong?"

Nonbeginning said, "Not understanding is the more profound position; understanding is comparatively shallow. Not understanding is being inside of Tao; understanding is looking at it from the outside."[5]

Great Clarity looked up and sighed. "So, claiming not to understand is really understanding, while claiming to understand is really not understanding. How can I ever get to a point where I understand this understanding of not understanding?"

(continued on page 123)

6 This rephrases the famous passage in the Tao-te-ching:

> *Look at it and do not see it: call it invisible.*
> *Listen to it and do not hear it: call it inaudible.*
> *Touch it and do not feel it: call it subtle.*
> *These three cannot be better understood:*
> *They merge and become one.*
> *Infinite and boundless:*
> *It cannot be named but belongs to no beings:*
> *the shape of no-shape, the form of no-form—*
> *Call it vague and obscure.*
> *Meet it, yet you cannot see its head,*
> *Follow it, yet you cannot see its back.* (chapter 14)

7 This is like being enlightened in Zen Buddhism. The state is so absorptive and nondual that the moment someone says, "I am enlightened," he or she is already creating a differentiation between the self, the state of enlightenment, and the words needed to formulate it. In other words, this person is certainly not enlightened, because anyone explaining the underlying oneness of the universe is not in fact completely one with it. Again, the Tao-te-ching: "The Tao that can be Tao'ed is not the eternal Tao. The name that can be named is not the eternal name" (chapter 1).

8 Trying to put a name to the eternal, to "Tao the Tao," means that you have no inner core, no feeling of connectedness to the cosmos. Instead you have a sense of limits in the outer world—which does not match reality, since the universe (and thus human potential) is without limit. You cannot truly appreciate the vastness of time and space and have no connection to cosmic beginning. This, then, will make it impossible to reach K'un-lun, the mythic paradise mountain of the immortals and world axis in Taoist cosmology, or make it impossible to wander about in emptiness, in mystical oneness with Tao.

Nonbeginning said, "Tao cannot be heard; if you hear it, it's not Tao. Tao cannot be seen; if you see it, it's not Tao. Tao cannot be spoken of; if you speak of it, it's not Tao. Understanding is just trying to give form to what is originally formless. In no way can Tao be named.[6]

"Anyone questioned about Tao who gives you an answer doesn't really understand it,[7] and anyone questioning Tao hasn't really heard of it yet.

"Tao is not to be questioned; and if questioned, there is no answer. Questioning the unquestionable is going to limits without; answering the unanswerable is having no core within. With no inner core trying to reach the limits without, such a person does not appreciate time and space on the outside, nor does he realize great beginning on the inside. Thus he will never make it to K'un-lun or get to wander about in emptiness."[8]

—CHAPTER 22

9 On the other hand, if it were possible to name and transmit Tao, people would do their best to pass it on to someone important to them—their rulers, their parents, their brothers and sisters, their children and grandchildren. It would be a very precious commodity that people would hasten to spread.

But it cannot be transferred; it is formless and beyond sensory and intellectual expressions, and so it can only be passed on—as the Zen tradition would say—from mind to mind. You have to have a certain level of inner purity, a certain sense of intuition, a certain steadiness and uprightness for the Tao to be received.

This is where withdrawal from society—at least for a period—and a quiet, reclusive lifestyle serve their purpose: to strengthen your inner qualities needed to receive and appreciate Tao and make it part of your life.

Lao-tzu said, "If Tao could be presented, everybody would immediately present it to their rulers. If it could be offered, everybody would immediately offer it to their parents. If it could be told, everybody would immediately tell it to their siblings. If it could be given, everybody would immediately give it to their children.

"But it cannot be any of these things. And the main reason is that unless there is steadiness in the person to receive it, it won't come to stay; unless there is uprightness in the person to activate it, it won't be possible to practice it.

"If whatever is released from within has no place to be received without, the sage will not release it. If whatever received from without has no steady place to stay within, the sage will not cherish it."**9**

—CHAPTER 14

10 The main figure in this dialogue is the Yellow Emperor, whom we already met as a culture hero who fought the first war, set up markets, and organized the government. That is his dominant Confucian image. In Taoist and longevity literature, he also frequently appears as a dedicated seeker. Thus, the main medical textbook of ancient China is the "Yellow Emperor's Inner Classic," where he asks questions that are answered by divinely inspired medical masters. The main sex manuals present a similar scenario: the Yellow Emperor is taught by various women, such as the Plain Woman (Sunü). Here he consults with Kuang-ch'eng-tzu (Guangchengzi) on how to attain immortality.

11 "Lying down," either on the back or on the side, as described in my *Chinese Healing Exercises*, was a key posture in traditional healing exercises (*tao-yin/daoyin*) and Taoist meditation before the arrival of Buddhism and its use of cross-legged sitting. The head being south, the master is looking to the north, facing the center of creativity in traditional cosmology. "Kneeling," with the buttocks on the backs of the legs, was the dominant posture of life in China until the Song dynasty (960–1260). As in Japan today, houses had thick mats, cushions, and low tables. Especially in formal situations and when approaching a lord, a person knelt, placed the hands on the floor, and "knocked the head to ground"—the literal translation of the word "kowtow."

12 The word for "eternal life" literally means "extended long time." The concept indicates immortality in the sense of oneness with Tao, a dissolution of personal identity in favor of the cosmos, an energetic transformation of individual vital energy into universal spirit. Since this transformation eliminates all mental tension and stress, oneness with Tao also means great health, vigor, and youthfulness as well as an extended life expectancy. It is often misunderstood, and even in traditional China inspired different schools, some of which also included physical practices not unlike yoga in the system.

The Yellow Emperor retired, left the world, set up a solitary hut, spread a plain mat, and went on retreat for three months. After that he visited the Master of Wide Accomplishments.[10] He found him lying down with his head to the south. In abject submission, the Yellow Emperor approached him on his knees, knocked his head to ground twice,[11] and asked, "I have heard that you have attained utmost Tao. May I ask what self-cultivation I should practice to reach eternal life?"[12]

(*continued on page 129*)

13 "Essence" indicates the central, core quality of something, the deepest within. "Ultimate" refers to the highest point, the most extreme, the vastest extension. The term is most familiar in the compound Great Ultimate (T'ai Chi/Taiji), which describes the world at the state of creation, as yin and yang are about to separate, and is often symbolized in the yin-yang diagram. In practice, it is activated in Tai Chi Chüan, "Great Ultimate Boxing," an unarmed martial art executed in slow motion that has profound meditative and health benefits.

The Tao in either dimension—essence and ultimate—has the characteristics of Chaos (Hun-tun): dark, murky, mystical, immersed, silent, serene. These, of course, also describe a deep trance or absorbed meditation.

14 Concrete practice instructions here relate back to oblivion: withdrawing the senses, holding the spirit, keeping things stable. "Clarity and stillness" is a technical term for meditation also mentioned in the Tao-te-ching that indicates the state of complete tranquility (stillness) within that will allow a sense of internal emptiness and the shining forth of a heavenly light (clarity). It is key to all later Taoist practice and the title of the most frequently chanted scripture today, the Ch'ing-ching-ching (Qingjing jing).

Another part of the practice is to maintain essence in the body. In Chinese medicine, essence is a subtle form of vital energy, the raw fuel that drives the pulsating rhythm of the body's cellular reproduction. Governed by the kidneys and the phase water, it is connected to primordial energy and determines a person's charisma, sexual attraction, and sense of wholeness. In its dominant form, essence is sexual potency: semen in men and menstrual blood in women, whose discharge is a major source of energy loss and should be avoided or controlled.

15 Unseeing and unhearing indicate the state of oblivion. This allows spirit—and thus Tao—to work unhindered in the person, causing the body to stay whole and healthy. It also means that you need to guard against sensory involvement and control outside involvements.

The Master got up quickly. "What a great question! Come and I will tell you all about utmost Tao. Its innermost essence is serene and obscure; its highest ultimate is murky and silent.[13]

"Practice being unseeing and unhearing, guard your spirit in stillness, and your body will automatically right itself.

"Practice stillness and clarity, never labor your body, never agitate your essence, and you can reach long life.[14]

"With your eyes unseeing, your ears unhearing, and your mind unknowing, your spirit will keep your body whole, and it will live forever. Protect your inner being, close off outside contacts—much knowledge leads to defeat.[15]

(continued on page 131)

16 A third aspect of Taoist immortality is ecstatic excursions to the far reaches of the cosmos, the source of yin and yang, heaven and earth. Adopting shamanic techniques of soul travel to the otherworld, Taoists use their mental and physical freedom to roam in cosmic spheres, such as the Heights of Great Radiance and the Gate of Serene Obscurity. Various divine beings (gods, immortals, perfected) reside in those far-off, supernatural places, beings who administer the world and control the movements of the planets. They are both created entities and aspects of Tao—higher in purity and subtler in energetic constellation than humans or animals. Oneness with Tao will transform a person into such a being—a major goal of Taoist religious practice.

17 "Guarding the One" is a technical term for meditation, often used together with "sitting in oblivion." It refers to a state of deep concentration and immersion in Tao and allows the adept to attain extensive longevity before reaching a position in the otherworld.

18 Once again, Tao is described as limitless and immeasurable, beyond all. Connected to it, you not only have health, vigor, and long life, but will also experience good fortune and positive situations in the world, coming to be a "king," that is, a person of high accomplishments. Disconnected from it, you remain on the "outside"—you may see the radiance of perfect happiness in the distance but remain in the dust, hampered by artificially created limits.

19 The Master here describes his ecstasy. He frolics in the limitless, moves about in infinity—the "Non-ultimate," the state before the Great Ultimate and after Chaos, when the world was all one, ready but not yet moving to be created. He joins the planets in their course and lives as long as heaven and earth, both images for the ecstatic freedom and eternal life to be experienced in the state of cosmic consciousness. In this way, he alone continues to survive.

"I will take you to the Heights of Great Radiance, the source of Utmost Yang. I will guide you through the Gate of Serene Obscurity, the source of Utmost Yin. This is where heaven and earth are administered, where yin and yang are being kept.[16]

"Protect your physical self, and things will naturally be vigorous. I constantly guard the One and rest in its deepest harmony. I have cultivated myself for twelve hundred years, and my body has yet to decay."[17]

Deeply impressed, the Yellow Emperor again knocked his head to ground. "You really are like heaven!"

"Come and I will tell you," the Master said. "That thing I have been talking about is limitless, yet people all think it has a limit. It is immeasurable, yet people all think it can be measured.

"Attaining Tao will make you a sovereign above and a king below. Losing Tao, you may see the light above but you'll remain mere dust below—like all the flourishing creatures that arise from dust and return to dust.[18]

"For this reason, I leave all that behind, go through the gate to the limitless, and frolic in the fields of infinity. I join my light with that of the sun and moon, extend my life span to that of heaven and earth. Things come near me—I remain with chaos. Things move away from me—I stay in oblivion. All others may well die—I alone survive!"[19]

—CHAPTER 11

20 In addition to the cosmic Tao, which is beyond time and space, there is also the Tao in the world. The text describes it in two areas: in the natural world and in society and politics.

In the natural world, the Tao is found everywhere—literally everywhere, even in trash and filth. Later Zen Buddhists picked up on this description, emphasizing that Buddha-nature is ubiquitous. The famous koan "Does this dog have Buddha-nature?" is a well-known expression of the concept.

For practitioners, this passage has two lessons. First, don't disregard anything because it appears to be lowly; even minor, apparently worthless and dirty things are Tao. And, Tao covers both extremes: the vastness of the universe and unlimited potential of creation as well as the concrete, daily, ordinary; it is in fact both, and we have to work with both.

21 There is no way to measure Tao as you would a pig—pushing deeper and into smaller recesses, trying to get to some core or depths. By the same token, words—even good ones, like "complete," "vast," and so on—will not do the trick. It is, to speak again in Zen metaphors, like the finger pointing at the moon: it just points, it is not the moon itself.

Master Eastwall asked Chuang-tzu, "What we call Tao, where is it?"

"There is no place where it is not."

"Can you be more specific?"

"It's in ants and crickets."

"How can it be so low?"

"It's in grass and weeds.

"But that's even lower!"

"It's in tiles and shards."

"Really, so very low?"

"It's in urine and feces."[20]

Master Eastwall did not respond.

Chuang-tzu said, "Your questions do not get to the heart of the matter. They are like a customer asking the market inspector about how to test the fat of a pig by stepping on it: the lower you go the more you learn. Don't look for any particular thing—nothing ever is without Tao! Utmost Tao is like this, and so are great words. 'Complete,' 'encompassing,' 'whole'—these three are different words that refer to the same reality; they all point to the One."[21]

—CHAPTER 22

22 Here we have yet another take on Tao in the world: its political and cultural dimension, presented in a list of classifications and social and political institutions. The sages of old put together systems that would make the Tao visible and active in the world. They created ethics and virtues, then set up social hierarchies and guidelines for proper behavior, followed by evaluations, rewards, and punishments.

The point here is that even these are all part of Tao. The same idea appears in a Taoist creation myth, documented in the fifth-century *K'ai-t'ien-ching* (*Kaitian jing*; Scripture on Cosmic Unfolding), where Lord Lao, the personified Tao, intentionally creates culture and institutions. In each successive age, he appears in visions to selected sages (like the prophets in ancient Israel) and gives them instructions on how to take the world to the next level. Taoism as a religion, in fact, emerged from such "revelations," given over many centuries and with varying content. In a dimension of Taoism often overlooked, religious leaders proposed political and social models to activate Tao in the world. On occasion, governments listened to them and instituted forms of Taoist administration.

23 The ultimate ideal is what the Chinese call Great Peace (*T'ai-p'ing*), a state of society where everyone works toward communal harmony with a great sense of cooperation, mutuality, and love. Chuang-tzu expresses this by saying that once the various institutions were in place, people knew who they were and what they were supposed to be doing; they all fulfilled their duties to perfection, behaved with obedience and care, and maintained good order everywhere.

The underlying belief here is that the Tao provides for all—everyone has his or her essential nature and original destiny, the perfect thing to do in the world and the right circumstances to do it in—and if everyone follows his or her inner Tao, the world is in complete alignment with Tao and functions perfectly. Government would not really be government, but just a relay system of coordination. Again, just as the perfection of knowledge is unknowing and the perfection of mind is no-mind, so the perfection of government is nongovernment.

In antiquity, those wanting to manifest Tao in the world first made sure that heaven was manifest, then virtuous ways came next.

Once virtuous ways were clear, benevolence and righteousness came next.

Once benevolence and righteousness were manifest, allotments and ranks came next.

Once allotments and ranks were manifest, positions and titles came next.

Once positions and titles were manifest, obedience and accord came next.

Once obedience and accord were manifest, inquiry and examination came next.

Once inquiry and examination were manifest, right and wrong came next.

Once right and wrong were manifest, rewards and punishments came next.[22]

Once rewards and punishments were manifest, the smart and dumb all knew what was what, and the VIPs and the nobodies all had their proper place—whether wise and kind or not so endowed, they all did their best.

Without fail, they had duties that matched their abilities and fulfilled the demands of their titles. This way, all served their superiors and took good care of their inferiors; they kept things in good order and cultivated themselves.

Never making use of external knowledge or fancy schemes, they reverted to their heavenly nature. This is what we call Great Peace. It is the utmost in government.[23]

—CHAPTER 13

1 What, then, would the ideal citizens of Great Peace, the perfected or sages, be like? How would their life be lived? What kind of attitudes would they display?

The first thing Chuang-tzu says is that the sage is heaven in action, which means all his or her doings are determined not by personal preferences or egoistic desires but are heaven and spirit working through the individual. By the same token, death to such a person is not the loss of a carefully crafted and ultimately artificial identity, but the mere change from one state of being to another, yet another transformation of many.

2 Being part of heaven, the sage matches yin and yang in rest and movement and relaxes into the flow of life, not worrying—like ordinary people do—about good fortune and bad luck. The sage only becomes active when circumstances require it and intuitively follows the course that is best for the greater good of the universe.

This, in turn, has the effect that there is no bad luck in such a person's life, but he or she naturally steps into good fortune. Rather than making a personal effort, the sage lets the Tao do the work. Western traditions have something very similar when they say, "Let go and let God." When you let things unfold naturally, the universe will provide.

3 Living with such an attitude, there is no need for planning or organizing, no need to push yourself forward. On the contrary, you can rest in your peace, stay radiant and self-confident. This, in turn, has an effect on health: you sleep undisturbed and wake cheerfully; there is nothing that will tire you out.

Again, this is an experience found in advanced meditators and spiritual people of many traditions. A good example is the centenarian Zen master whose body may be fragile but who does not slow down: sharp as a whip, he is going strong; his mind focused and free, he never fatigues.

10 ☐ The Perfected

The life of the sage is heaven in action; the death of the sage is being transformed.**1**

In stillness, her inherent potency matches yin; in motion, her flow matches yang. She does nothing to initiate good fortune; nothing to anticipate calamity.

She gets an impulse, only then responds; receives a push, only then gets going; finds no other way, and only then stirs herself.

Giving up analysis and precedents, she intuitively follows the inherent order of the cosmos. For this reason, she is completely free from all natural disasters, attachments to things, opposition from others, and spiritual burdens.**2**

Her life is a smooth flow; her death a welcome respite. She never thinks or worries, plans or organizes.

Full of radiance, she never shines bright; full of confidence, she never expects much.

She sleeps without dreaming and wakes without concern. Her spirit is pure and simple; her spirit soul never tires.

In emptiness and nonbeing, peace and serenity, she fully matches the inherent potency of heaven.**3**

—Chapter 15

4 The word "perfected" translates *chen-jen* (*zhenren*), which has been rendered variously as "true man," "authentic persons," "genuine human being," "a real mensch." The English word "perfected" implies a twofold dimension that is key to understanding the Taoist vision: the connection to the original perfection of Tao at the root of creation and the effort-based unfolding of a new level of perfection, a new evolutionary stage in the development of humanity.

5 Content with whatever is, being fully present in the present moment, such people accept reality as it is. If things go wrong, they deal with it; if things go well, they deal with it. They do not make major emotional investments one way or the other and are in fact "without feelings." In addition, they don't worry about problems; they may encounter high places, water, and fire—elements that can harm people—but will survive without a scratch.

The phrase is both metaphorical and literal: people whose minds are whole or who are in a state of deep absorption or ecstatic trance indeed survive being immersed in water or walking over hot coals. The human mind is immensely strong when it comes to preventing or inviting injury to the body.

6 Here is a brief reference to concrete practice: the perfected breathe to the heels as opposed to the chest. Healthy and spiritually strong people stand tall and breathe with their bellies, guiding breath and thus vital energy all the way through the body. Ordinary people, on the other hand, have abdominal muscles tightened by fear, rounded shoulders bent forward for protection, and sunken chests—all physical signs of stress. They cannot breathe properly, which in turn intensifies their tension and increases the flow of adrenaline.

7 Being at rest with themselves, the perfected accept all as it comes, not loving life or hating death, but letting go of all preconception and just moving along with the world. They let heaven and Tao do what they do best and do not try to help them along.

What, then, are the perfected?**4**

The perfected of old did not resent being humble, did not take pride in success, and never plotted their affairs. From this basis, they could be without regret if things went wrong, remain free from self-congratulation when they went right.

For this reason, they could climb high places without getting scared, dive into water without getting soaked, and pass through fire without getting hot.**5** Their understanding was such that they could rise up and join Tao at all times.

The perfected of old slept without dreaming and woke without concerns. Their food was plain and their breath deep. In fact, the perfected breathes all the way to the heels while the multitude breathe just to the throat—bent over and submissive, they croak out words as if they were retching; full of intense passions and desires, they have only the thinnest connection to heaven.**6**

The perfected of old had no clue about loving life and hating death. They came to life without celebration; they left again without messiness. Calmly they came, calmly they went—and that is all. They never forgot where they came from; they never inquired about where they would end. They received whatever came and enjoyed it; they lost whatever went and just let it go.

This way of being in the world is called not using the mind to oppose Tao, not using human faculties to assist heaven. This, indeed, is what the perfected are like.**7**

—CHAPTER 6

8 | The effect of such a person in society is tremendous. A wonderful illustration appears in a Zen story made into a movie and retold by Janwillem van de Wetering in *The Empty Mirror*.

According to this story, two petty thieves, an old beggar couple, a stuttering idiot, and a prostitute occupy a ramshackle house in an inner-city slum. A wandering monk, a bald old man with only a staff and bowl, asks for shelter, and they agree to put him up as a sign of good luck. He sits down in a corner while the inhabitants argue about whose turn it is to clean up. As soon as he realizes what the problem is, he gets up and does the job.

As time goes on, the monk continues to be fully present in the moment and do whatever needs to be done as required by circumstances. By just being there, polite and friendly, he gradually turns the house around. He helps. When the old invalid dies, the monk holds his hand. When the idiot cannot find his flute, he discovers it for him. He never criticizes, never praises. When the burglars get jobs as laborers, he says nothing. When the prostitute becomes a cleaning woman, he merely smiles. The story ends with a New Year's party. Everyone contributes and all join in the fun. Honesty, harmony, and care prevail where discord had been the norm.

In a more modern, scientific context, David R. Hawkins, in *Power vs. Force: The Hidden Determinants of Human Behavior*, notes that a single person at a high level of spiritual evolution (fully at one with love, peace, and enlightenment) has a major transformative effect on the combined consciousness of the planet and can make up for as many as seventy thousand people in survival mode (tormented by desires and pushing for apparent success).

He also claims that, based on kinesiological testing, humanity as a whole has recently passed the critical threshold of "courage," so that as a species we are starting to go beyond negative reactions and move forward into positive community building. A related movement is Consciousness Convergence, which encourages people to enhance their minds into cosmic mode both individually and in group practice.

The sage, when in poverty, makes his family forget their dire needs; when in success, causes kings and dukes to forget their rank and income, causing them to be humble.

His way of relating to other creatures is to share his pleasures with them; his way of relating to other people is to be happy to connect to them while keeping himself whole.

Without a word he brings harmony to people. Just standing by them, he encourages them to improve—quite like a father would do with his son.

Resting quietly at home, he is immersed in leisure yet immensely active. He could not be farther away from the minds of ordinary people![8]

—CHAPTER 25

9 Relaxing into the flow of things and being fully present, however, does not mean total passivity. As sages and the perfected live in the world and support it, they act in accordance with high moral standards—fulfilling the classical virtues but without conscious effort or making a big deal of them.

This connects to the conviction that Tao as cosmic flow is inherently good but not essentially moral. The cosmos and nature are cruel and unjust at times; they do not have a set of values that can be defined or to which they can be held. At the same time, the goodness of the cosmos is intuited by human beings as a sense of well-being and inner harmony that, if it is to be achieved with limited sensory and intellectual faculties, can be expressed in moral rules. Morality is thus part of the cosmic harmony that Taoists embody, and their being in the world increases the ethical quality of life around them. Nevertheless, perfected Taoists are not moral per se, but rather transmoral or supramoral, going beyond human society yet spontaneously doing what is best for it.

10 Thus the sage as citizen obeys all the laws and observes all social conventions; as a member of the government, she takes care of others and does her best for them. Accomplished Taoists are always also political figures; the qualities that allow them to transform the society around them also make them prime candidates for political power—how much better would the world be if a person of high integrity and enlightenment were to lead it? The inner qualities filter down and have a transformative effect. For this reason Taoists of all ages propose mystics as rulers and encourage rulers to train in Tao.

11 This summarizes the sage's conundrum, the conflict between embodiment and transcendence: born and alive in a body and in human society, she is a "being among beings," yet in her mind and heart she is far beyond ordinary people. So she is essentially free from the world and could just sit in a cave and do nothing. However, she is also part of the world and "cannot not act." Being human means being socially responsible, and thus a sage is impelled to work for the world.

Thus the sage
observes heaven but does not assist it;
fulfills his inherent potential but does not get attached to it;
lives in Tao but does not plan for it;
acts with benevolence but does not revere it;
is full of social responsibility but does not make it a duty.[9]
The sage
accords with propriety without ever violating its rules;
takes care of affairs without ever making excuses;
follows the law without ever creating disorder;
cherishes the people without ever taking them lightly;
does his best for others without ever dismissing them.[10]
Although a being among beings, she is yet essentially free from the need
to act in the world—however, she cannot not act.[11]

—CHAPTER 11

12 The perfected thus stick to the basics, acting socially responsible and making do with whatever heaven and life have to offer. They observe social and legal rules but are not tied to them; they are laid-back and "empty" but don't make a show of it.

They may be found in all levels of society—humble yet cheerful, eminent yet natural. Their vital energy collected within, they give a good presentation of proper behavior; their vital energy flowing to others, they yet know when to stop, staying within the limits of what they can do.

13 They can be open-minded and appear like others, but they are also complete in themselves and reach far beyond ordinary levels. Their minds inwardly connected or "linked in," they seem to be fond of their free time and like to relax; their minds emptied or "spaced out," they seem distracted and not quite there.

14 With all these characteristics, the perfected also take an active role in society. If influential in government, they accept the need for punishments but are careful in their application. They acknowledge the importance of social conventions and make sure to observe them. They use their wisdom and intuition to feel the pulse of events and ensure things are done at the right time, never putting a personal agenda ahead of what is needed for the greater good. And they keep within the boundaries of their inherent potency, realizing at all times what they can and cannot do and taking things one step at a time.

The perfected of old maintained social responsibility and never waivered, accepting nothing even when in dire straits. They were dedicated to observing the rules but not rigid about them; extensive in their emptiness but not fanciful with it.

Humble and withdrawing, they were always cheerful; eminent and superior, they gave themselves no airs. Collected, they knew how to present a proper demeanor; outgoing, they knew when to stop within the range of their inherent potency.[12]

Open-minded, they seemed to be just like everyone else; self-contained, they yet went beyond all constraints. Linked in, they seemed like they enjoyed a bit of leisure; spaced out, they forgot what they were trying to say.[13]

They considered punishments as the substance [of government], propriety as its supporting wings, wisdom as the key to good timing, and inherent potency as its main guideline.

Punishments as substance means being lenient in the infliction of death; propriety as supporting wings means behaving with care in the world; wisdom as key to good timing means not elevating personal causes above the needs of affairs; and inherent potency as the main guideline means taking things one step at a time to get up the hill.[14]

—CHAPTER 6

15 What, then, are some of the techniques to get closer to the sagely or perfected state? The first step is to realize that self-realization is more important than success, wealth, or status. What the world may think is the height of achievement, what your parents would like you to be, may be completely wrong for you. Finding value in yourself, discovering what gives you greatest joy and most fulfillment is essential. This leads to perfect happiness and the state of perfection.

Best-selling author Gary Zukav calls it "authentic power" in his book *Soul Stories*. He says, "Authentic power feels good. It is doing what you are supposed to be doing. It is fulfilling. Your life is filled with meaning and purpose. You have no doubts. You have no fears. You are happy to be alive. You have a reason to be alive. Everything you do is joyful. Everything is exciting.... You are not worried about doing something wrong, making a mistake, or failing. You do not compare yourself with others. You do not compare what you do with what others do."

16 Does this mean lots of work on self-cultivation? The need for books and teachings, workshops and retreats? Yes and no. They certainly help, especially in a society that is so full of opportunities and information as ours, where distractions are manifold and demands can be excessive. It is hard to quiet down enough, to listen for the right signs and figure out who you really are and what you do best.

On the other hand, none of these cultivation practices are really necessary; the inner urge to do what you are best at can be so strong that "there is absolutely nothing that could separate [you] from it."

Lao-tzu said, "Once you understand that the value of the self is higher than any career, you can give up position and income like shaking off mud. Finding value in yourself and never losing this under any circumstances makes it possible to flow along with the myriad transformations without end. Then, what could possibly cause you any distress? The more you act in Tao, the clearer this becomes."[15]

Confucius responded, "Your inherent potency matches that of heaven and earth, yet you still use abstract terms and cultivate your mind. Who, even among the superior men of old, could ever do without them?"

"Not quite. When water flows downward, it doesn't *do* anything but just follows its inherent nature. Similarly, when the utmost person fulfills his inherent potency, he does not cultivate anything and yet there is absolutely nothing that could separate him from it. It is just as the sky is naturally high, earth is naturally solid, the sun and the moon are naturally bright—what is there to cultivate?"[16]

—CHAPTER 21

17 This closely echoes the Tao-te-ching chapter entitled "Can You?"

> Containing vital energy and embracing oneness, can you
>   prevent it from leaving?
> Concentrating on the breath and attaining softness, can you
>   be like an infant?
> Purifying and cleansing your mysterious perception, can
>   you be without error?
> Then you will be free from lasciviousness and wrongdoing.
> As the Gate of Heaven opens and shuts, can you be like the
>   female?
> Brightly penetrating the four quarters, can you be without
>   knowledge?
> Be creative and cultivate things; be creative but do not
>   strive to own them.
> Act without dependence; excel but do not push.
> This is called mysterious potency. (chapter 10)

The practice is to stop, to let go, to release; it is the conscious rejection of the masculine, alpha-personality-type drive for success, replacing it with the more feminine, restful way of being, in a state of softness and quietude.

It also is the meditative effort of keeping vital energy in the body and holding on to single-minded concentration, of focusing on the breath and creating a state of detached mindfulness—precursors to the deeper trance states that lead to oblivion.

18 The goal, then, is to recover the qualities of a baby: to be able to cry, clench the hands, and stare at one spot all day long without ever getting physically tired, strained, or exhausted. There is harmony within, a strong sense of inherent potency, and the power to remain focused in meditative oblivion and free from distractions. This leads to wholeness, to a connection with inner aspects of Tao, and thus to perfection—and also to the preservation of health and long life.

Lao-tzu said: The way of preserving life—here it is:

Can you embrace oneness?

Can you stick to it and never let it go?

Can you understand good and bad fortune without divination?

Can you stop?

Can you let be?

Can you let go of all others and concentrate just on yourself?

Can you be calm?

Can you be dumb?[17]

Can you be like an infant?

An infant cries all day long, and its throat never gets hoarse—it has total harmony.

It balls its fingers into a fist all day long, and its hand never lets go—it matches inherent potency.

It stares at one point all day long and never once blinks—it has no outside distractions.[18]

In the same way: walk without knowing where you're going, rest without realizing what you're doing, join others in their activities and flow along with their motions—this is the way of preserving life.

—CHAPTER 23

The New Life

1 Useful and useless are worldly categories that require goals and purposes for definition. One of the key things the aspiring Taoist sage has to learn is acceptance of uselessness in the terms of the world. What his or her best ability and destiny suggest to do may be far out, unproductive, and of low esteem. Still, in the greater framework of the cosmos, even things and people who are apparently useless have their use, such as artists who create beauty or ascetics whose moral and mental purity enhances the sum total of planetary consciousness.

2 The Yellow Springs, called Yomi in Japanese Shinto, are the oldest recorded underworld in the Far East, a realm of the dead not unlike Hades in ancient Greece. People's spirit souls would go there to reside as ancestors, supervised by an otherworldly administration. The dead stayed in active contact with the living, watched over them, and received their offerings. It was also believed possible to reach the Yellow Springs if one dug far enough into the earth.

3 The small space we occupy on the planet is so important to us, yet it can be made useless quite easily if taken up by other projects. To see things in their proper perspective, it is important to understand them in various levels of relationship and to appreciate them from different perspectives.

Useful and useless as categories shift quite easily: what may be useless to one person quite possibly is highly useful to another; what may appear useless today may turn out to be very useful tomorrow, and vice versa.

11 □ Uselessness

Hui-tzu said to Chuang-tzu, "Tell me about the useless."[1]

"Once you understand the useless, that's when you're ready to start talking about the useful. For example, heaven and earth are expansive and huge everywhere, but any individual only uses enough to put his feet on. If, however, you dug deep right around someone's feet, reaching all the way to the Yellow Springs—would the spot still be useful?"[2]

"No, it would be useless."

"So, in this case, the useless greatly clarifies what it means to be useful."[3]

—CHAPTER 26

4 Fortune-telling by looking at facial features and the bone structure of the skull is called physiognomy. It was widely practiced in ancient China, focusing particularly on the nose, lips, and forehead.

5 What seems unfortunate or useless to one may be fortunate or useful to another. The diviner says K'un will be fortunate in that he gets to eat at a lord's table, but for his father being too close to the aristocracy cannot be a good thing. It is all in the eye of the beholder.

6 Just as eunuchs—men whose genitalia had been amputated—were used widely as servants in the women's quarters of the imperial court and feudal lords, so people who had lost a foot or were otherwise maimed were useful as gatekeepers, since they could not desert their posts and run away.

7 While it was terribly unfortunate that he lost his foot, K'un nevertheless was fortunate in that he obtained a good position and shared a lord's table for many years. What seemed useless or terrible in the beginning turned out to be useful and quite acceptable. The point is that when things happen to us in life—due to circumstances and our own inherent tendencies—even if they seem terrible at the time, we don't know what they may be good for in the long run.

Tzu-ch'i (Ziqi) had eight sons. He asked them all to line up before him, then called in the fortune-teller Yen of the Nine Directions. "Please check out the looks of my sons for me: who among them will be most fortunate?"[4]

"K'un will be most fortunate."

Tzu-ch'i was surprised and delighted: "How so?"

"Well, K'un here, he will join the meals of a noble lord until the end of his days."

Hearing this, Tzu-ch'i was distressed and burst into tears. "Why would a son of mine ever get to such an extreme?"...[5]

Not long after this, Tzu-ch'i sent K'un to go to the state of Yen. On the road, he was captured by bandits. They figured he would be hard to sell as an able-bodied man, but when maimed would make an easy sale.[6] So they cut off his foot and sold him to the government of Ch'i (Qi), where he became gatekeeper for Duke K'ang—and was eating meat until the end of his days.[7]

—Chapter 24

8 East Asian religions venerate the earth as sacred and have various deities for all kinds of natural phenomena, including dragons who manage rivers, lakes, and oceans; mountain gods; thunder deities; and so on. One of the most ancient deities is the earth god, a formless spirit, worshiped at nature altars, which were open-air mounds marked by large stones and planted with trees matching cosmic *ch'i*. Big trees very commonly were venerated as representatives of the earth god— as they are still in Japan today, where they are marked with holy ropes and given various offerings.

Some shrines were more popular than others; those that had a particularly large tree and were easily accessible might attract large numbers of worshipers as well as vendors and popular entertainment, creating a scene like a popular market.

9 The tree is "disintegrating"—the word used is *san*, which means "scatter" or "disperse." It is also used to describe the action of *ch'i* in life and death: it comes together or assembles, and there is life; it "disperses" or disintegrates, and there is death. In other words, the *ch'i* in this tree is not focused; it is energetically spread out. Thus its wood has no solidity or permanence and cannot be used for timber.

Being entirely useless for all ordinary, practical purposes is yet highly useful to the tree, which reached a great old age due to its very uselessness and could serve as a focus for the spirits.

Carpenter Shih traveled to Ch'i and arrived in Twisted Axle. There he saw an oak serving as an earth-god shrine. Its canopy could cover several thousand oxen, and it had a circumference of a hundred spans. Towering over the hillside, its lowest branches started at about eighty feet, several tens of them so huge they could easily be made into boats. Sightseers flocked to it as if it were a popular market.[8]

The carpenter ignored it, pursuing his path without stopping. However, his assistant observed it with admiration, then ran to catch up with his master. He said, "Ever since I picked up my axe and chisel and became your disciple, I have never seen timber as beautiful as this. Now, you don't even look at it but pass by it without stopping. Why?"

"Off with you," Shih replied. "Don't even talk about it. It's a disintegrating tree. Make it into a boat—it sinks; make it into a coffin or chest—it rots; make it into a table—it collapses; make it into a door—it leaks sap; make it into a pillar—it's riddled with insects. This is not a timber tree. There's nothing it can be used for—that's why it could reach such a great age."[9]

(continued on page 159)

10 The downside of being useful is that it invites abuse: the moment you have something other people find useful, they pounce on you and make you do things you do not really want to do. This in turn leads to suffering and a shortened life expectancy. However, this pattern is so common that somehow you get used to it and think that this is how life should be, subconsciously inviting the abusive pattern to continue.

11 The greatest use of uselessness is to stay alive and whole. Nobody raids you, nobody makes you do things you don't want to do, nobody limits your potential by pushing you into a certain niche that makes you "useful" to society.

In addition, understanding uselessness as potentially useful remedies the arrogance of humanity toward nature and objects. The tree here is a living thing that—like the skull in an earlier story—can appear to people in dreams and is essentially on the same footing. The story makes the point very clearly: everything created is by nature "disintegrating," in a state of entropy, getting closer to death, and thus we have no right to judge other people or beings or even things in terms of being useless or useful. It is much better to see everything in its own right.

12 Seeing everything in its own right, we no longer use ordinary standards or measurements to judge things but accept them as they are. And then, it turns out, even the apparently most useless can find its place in the greater scheme of things, just as the big tree has found a use in the world as a spirit habitation. Still, it takes this purpose on only as a temporary measure, having quite different values—like the perfected, it cannot be measured by ordinary yardsticks.

On his return journey, Carpenter Shih again passed through the town. The earth-god tree appeared to him in a dream and said:

"What can you possibly compare me to? You want to compare me to a cultivated tree? Let's look at them—cherry, pear, orange, grapefruit, and all those other fruit trees: as soon as their fruits are ripe, they are knocked down and thrown into the dirt. Their big limbs are broken, their small branches torn. Thus they suffer through life and do not complete their heaven-given years, dying prematurely in mid-stride, yet constantly ready to receive more abuse from the world.[10]

"The same holds true for all things. For the longest time, I tried to find out if there wasn't something I could possibly be used for. I almost died in the process, but now I realize that this very uselessness has been my greatest use. Just assume I had had some use for people—how could I ever have grown so huge? Plus, you and I are both created things— how can a mere thing pass judgment on another? You're just a disintegrating person getting closer to death—what do you really know about a disintegrating tree?"[11]

After waking, Carpenter Shih related his dream. His disciple commented, "Being so keen on uselessness, why does it serve as an earth-god shrine?"

"Shut up! Don't say a word! It is merely resting here for a while, thinking of the ignorant crowd as a curse. Also, if it did not serve as an earth-god shrine, someone would have a go at it. Really, you must see that what it values is quite different from that of the masses—using common measures like social responsibility to compare it, how absurd is that?"[12]

—CHAPTER 4

13 Here is another example of a perfectly useless creature that yet has its place in the greater scheme of things and for its very uselessness manages to survive intact and without afflictions.

This, then, would be what the life of the sage might be like— unless his essential nature and destiny demand some other action, his behavior in the world would be like that of the Lazy Brain bird: being useless and content with what there is, moving only when pushed, resting only when comfortable, and thereby escaping all harm.

There's a bird in the Eastern Sea called Lazy Brain. It fluffs and flutters about as if it had no strength, flies only when pulled and supported, and roosts only when squeezed and pressed. When the flock moves out, it never takes the lead; when the flock retreats, it never is in the rear. In feeding, it never takes the first bite and is content to eat what's left behind. For this reason, its progress is not broken, other creatures and people will not harm it, and it escapes from afflictions.[13]

—CHAPTER 20

14 However, we cannot always just be withdrawing and useless. There are various dimensions of uselessness—while it may be lifesaving in one case, it can be potentially disastrous in another. Where, then, should the sage place himself? What should we aspire to? Be useless for practical purposes but have a spiritual position—like the giant tree that serves as an earth-god shrine? Or be useful but on the fringes of things so as not to be involved? Where should we place ourselves?

15 Trying to stay in the realm between the useful and the useless is tricky because we still have to operate within the categories of the world and continuously check on developments and balance positions and behaviors. Since things unfold and times change, we may never be quite certain which is which and, as a result, get terribly involved, worried, and concerned.

16 The answer, then, is to reach a state of free and easy wandering, connected to Tao and living fully within the realm of inherent potency, realizing our inborn potential without rigidity. We move along with the times, allow changes to happen, follow the demands of our inherent gifts and of the needs of society around us. Floating freely, in constant intuitive touch with Tao—the ancestor of things—we let things be and stay beyond all involvements and entanglements.

This does not mean being a Lazy Brain. It means appearing to be a Lazy Brain but being active according to our best abilities, serving as a catalyst so everyone—and by extension, the world—can be his or her best.

Chuang-tzu and his disciple were walking in the mountains when they saw a huge tree with thick branches and luxuriant foliage. A woodcutter stood next to it but would not touch it. Chuang-tzu asked him why.

"There's nothing it can be used for."

"Because it does not have any practical use, this tree can live out its heaven-given years," was Chuang-tzu's comment.

Having left the mountain, they lodged in the house of an old friend. Happy to have them, he ordered his houseboy to get a goose for dinner. The boy said, "One of the geese can cackle, the other can't—which should I kill?"

"Kill the one that cannot cackle," the host decided.

The following day, the disciple asked, "Yesterday we saw a tree on the mountain that can live out its heaven-given years because it does not have any practical use. Today we are faced with the goose of our host that is being killed because it does not have any practical use. Which position would you prefer?"[14]

Chuang-tzu laughed. "At first glance, I would prefer to be in a position between having and not having a practical use. Being between the two seems to be right, but it really wouldn't be, since I could never get out of entanglements.[15]

"This, however, could be avoided if I simply hitched myself on Tao and inherent potency, floating and wandering freely. I would be above praise and blame, now a dragon, then a snake. I would change in accordance with the times, never willing to stick to one thing. Now high, then low, harmony would be my core. Floating and wandering with the ancestor of the myriad things, I treat things as things but won't be treated as one myself. So how would I ever get hooked up with entanglements?"[16]

—CHAPTER 20

17 Living to the fullest and realizing our abilities, we must also deal with all things in the world, seeing their inherent potential and making the best of them. Even a huge gourd has its uses, but Hui-tzu cannot see them. His imagination is limited; his perspective is constrained—he tries to use the gourd for ordinary purposes, as a water barrel or a ladle, and when that does not work, he gets rid of it. He is not making the best of what he is given.

18 Another example of the same kind is the recipe for chapped hands. One recipe, yet how different its uses—in a family business and a royal campaign—and with what different effects and rewards.

The thing is the same, but what you do with it differs. You can use anything in an ordinary, limited way, following tradition and sticking to the boundaries. Or you can look at it with creative imagination and go far beyond, making a difference to yourself and the world. We all have a certain amount of time to spend on the planet, but what we do with it is vastly different.

19 The trick is to see the potential of things and make the most of them, in this case realizing that the huge gourd could be used for boating. To see this we have to keep our mind simple and unencumbered, and the answer will come of itself.

Similarly, use what you have in life and enjoy it in the best possible way, recognizing your gifts, your inborn potential, and the chances the world offers. The Chuang-tzu expresses this in the concept of natural skills.

Hui-tzu said to Chuang-tzu, "The king of Wei gave me seeds for a big gourd. I planted them and they grew into this gigantic thing that could hold fifty gallons. I filled it with water, but it got so heavy I could not lift it. I cut it in two for ladles, but their dippers were sunk and they didn't hold anything. It had nothing going for it except its humongous size, so I figured it was totally useless and smashed it to pieces."[17]

"Oh my, what an idiot you are when it comes to using big things!

"Let me tell you. There was this guy from Song who produced a great ointment to prevent chapped hands, and for generations his family made it their business to bleach silk [in hot water]. A passerby heard about it and proposed to buy the recipe for a hundred dollars.

"The clan gathered and deliberated. 'For generations,' they agreed, 'we have been bleaching silk and never made more than a few bucks. Now we can sell the technique and make a hundred in a single morning—let's give it to him.'

"The man took the prescription and immediately went to talk to the king of Wu, who at the time had trouble with the state of Yüeh. The king made him a general, and in the following winter he fought a naval battle against Yüeh, defeating it thoroughly. He was duly given a nice parcel of the conquered land.

"In both cases the key to success was the ability to prevent chapped hands. But in one it led to a substantial land grant; in the other it resulted in the continuation of a simple silk-bleaching business. The difference is all in the use.[18]

"Now you, my friend, had a gourd large enough to hold fifty gallons. Why did you not think of making it into a big tub and float around the rivers and lakes instead of worrying about the dippers being sunk and not holding anything? Really, you still have such an overgrown mind!"[19]

—CHAPTER 1

1 Whatever the outside circumstances may be and whatever destiny has in store, there is a core within all people that guides them to do what they do best and what brings them most fulfillment. These are the natural skills, the inherent potency made concrete.

Possessions and fame—material goods and public success—are outside goals that are achieved only at the cost of losing our integrity, giving up what makes us happiest in day-to-day life.

Most people, however, are lured into going after outside goals and thereby lose "heaven," their natural inclinations, the things they do best and that give them the most satisfaction. An example would be if a naturally gifted musician or artist sets her sights on becoming a lawyer or corporate executive—giving up her inner core for something society deems desirable.

2 The best way of acting in the world is to never mind classifications and values established by tradition (crooked and straight, right and wrong) and just follow your natural inclination. Pursue "heaven," your true gifts and most satisfying activities, to its limit, doing whatever it takes to realize it by working within the given circumstances. Hold on to the "central pivot," your soul or inner core, which will give you a good intuitive sense of what is right for you.

Realize that it is impossible for you to be like anyone else: cherish your aloneness, your uniqueness, and follow your inherent intention— what your inner self tells you is best. This way, you will be on the right path without going back and forth, you will be naturally righteous or socially responsible, and you may even become rich and famous—but that would be coincidental and should not be the primary goal.

12 □ Natural Skills

The little people desperately run after possessions; those at the top desperately run after fame. They differ in the exact way in which they betray their integrity and alter their essential nature, but they are quite the same in that they throw away what is already theirs and desperately run after something that is not.

Thus we say:

Don't be like the little people—hold on to heaven and do all you can to realize it. Don't be like those at the top—just follow the cosmic order of heaven.[1]

Don't mind whether anything is crooked or straight—just pursue heaven to its limit. Do what you need to do in the four directions and go along with the times.

Don't mind whether anything is right or wrong—just hold on to the central pivot within. Cherishing your aloneness, fulfill your intentions and ramble about with Tao.

Follow your path without turning, be righteous without trying—lest you lose what is originally yours. Don't pursue riches, don't run after success—lest you discard heaven.[2]

—CHAPTER 29

3 "Simply divine" means that someone does something as if divinely inspired, as if the person's spirit or the gods—in classical Chinese expressed by the same word as "divine"—were working through the person. It is what you do with joy, effortlessly, simply, and with perfect timing. This is what a natural skill, an inherent quality, properly trained and developed, looks like.

4 The people who handle boats best are those who are natural on the water or in the water. For them, water is their natural element. It is not special, awesome, or threatening, but just the place where they feel most at home. In their element, any event can be handled with ease and perfect competence.

The "inner space" is the intuitive center within, the central pivot of the previous passage. It is expressed with the term *she*, which means "lodge" or "resting place." Often the body is described as a lodge of the spirit. Similarly, here the intuitive center of the person in his or her right element is the lodge of competence and security. Based on this center, we can be at ease everywhere and under any circumstances.

5 This gives a good example of what is meant by pursuing outside things instead of focusing on your natural skill and inner satisfaction. Wanting something badly means that you are directing energy outside and the more you do so, the less secure you are within, which in turn results in decreased competence and lack of success. It is, in other words, better to do things for the sake of doing them than for some outside reward.

Yen-yüan (Yanyuan) was talking to Confucius. "The other day I crossed the gulf of Goblet Depth, and the ferryman was simply divine in running the boat.[3] I asked him, 'Is it possible to learn to run a boat like this?' He said, 'Sure. Lots of people can if they are good on the water. And for those good at diving—well, they may never even have seen a boat, but they can run it to perfection.' I asked him for details, but he wouldn't say any more. Could you explain what he meant?"

"'Lots of people can if they are good on the water'—that means water is their natural element and they are completely oblivious of it. 'And for those good at diving—well, they may never have seen a boat, but they can run it perfectly'—that means for them water is just as solid as dry ground, and if a boat capsizes, it is like a cart overturning.

"Capsizing, overturning, whatever—a myriad different events may come right at them and yet they will never let them disturb their inner space. How could they go anywhere and not be at ease?[4]

"If you join a contest and shoot to win a nice brick, you will be skillful. If you shoot for a fancy buckle, you will be nervous. If you shoot for a gold bar, you will be a wreck.

"Your shooting skill is the same in all cases, but if there is something you want badly, your focus will be outside. And the more your focus is outside, the more you get clumsy on the inside."[5]

—CHAPTER 19

6 This story gives an example of the practical application of this idea in cookery. The perfect cook has movements that are so finely coordinated it is as if he were moving to music in a kind of wondrous dance. And just as when letting go in a dance, when music takes over body and consciousness, the cook here moves along with something greater, more harmonious. It is far beyond mere skill—it is the alignment of self and Tao, the working of spirit through the self.

7 As the cook develops his skill, he moves through phases that match the method of mind fasting described earlier. He first sees solid reality, which has names and divisions and is perceived with the senses. Then he lets go of that and starts seeing more subtle patterns, using the mind and pure perception to relate to the ox. Finally, he overcomes this level and abandons all sensory and conscious categories, going purely with intuition, feeling the *ch'i* of things, and letting spirit move.

8 The spirit takes over, and you can go along freely with the patterns set up in nature. Then you can do any job with panache and in perfect relaxation, in comfort and with ease, yet powerfully efficient and without error.

Cook Ting (Ding) was carving up an ox for Lord Wen-hui. His hands were touching, his shoulders leaning, his feet stepping, his knees thrusting—each with its own sound, all knife cuts completely in tune, as if he were performing the dance Mulberry Forest or moving to the tune "Commanding Chief."[6]

Lord Wen-hui said, "Wow! This is great! How did you ever get to be so good at this?"

Cook Ting put down his knife and turned to him.

"What I really love is Tao, which goes way beyond skill. When I first started carving oxen, I saw nothing but the ox as a solid thing. After three years I stopped seeing it as an entity, and nowadays I use my spirit when I approach it and don't even see it with my eyes at all.[7]

"As I stop using my senses and conscious awareness, the spirit takes over completely. It lets me follow the natural contours, twisting in the deep hollows, sliding through the great openings. Thus I go along with the structure of the ox, naturally avoiding arteries and tendons and certainly all the big joints.[8]

(continued on page 173)

9 If we use things the wrong way, without inspiration, they won't last very long—knives are blunted, bodies tire, shoes get worn out. The idea here is the same as that of the baby in an earlier chapter: it can cry or ball its hands into fists all day long without getting tired. The spirit moves and all implements, including the body, never tire. This is also why Taoists can live such long and healthy lives—there is nothing that could harm their bodies, and healing takes places naturally as life flows along.

10 Sometimes, however, things may get a bit tricky. Then it is important to use the senses and the physical body with great focus and good care. Moving very slowly, keeping our concentration powerful, so that the spirit has room to move, we proceed with infinite caution. This, then, leads to a point where even a very minor action can resolve the situation, and problem areas unravel as if by magic. Again, Tao is allowed to flow.

11 The entire story, moreover, is a parable for nourishing life. We can apply the skills of the cook to living the best, longest, and healthiest life possible. Focusing on the task at hand, letting go of all other concerns, and moving along with the nooks and crannies of day-to-day reality, we nourish life fully.

"A good cook needs to change his knife every year, because he cuts. An ordinary cook needs to change his knife every month, because he hacks. I have had this knife for nineteen years. I have carved several thousand oxen with it, yet its edge is as thin as if it had just come from the whetstone.

"There are spaces between the joints, and with a thin knife edge I can get in there. With a blade so thin, there's plenty of room to move about, and even some to spare! Thus I have been able to use the same knife for nineteen years and it's still as good as new.[9]

"Nevertheless, whenever I come to a complicated joint and see that it will be difficult, I proceed with great caution, focus my vision, and move very slowly. I only make the slightest movements of the knife, and the part quickly separates, dropping like a clod of earth.[10] Then I raise the knife and I stand tall, looking all around in complete satisfaction. Eventually I wipe the knife and store it away."

Lord Wen-hui said, "Wonderful! I have listened to Cook Ting speak about his work and learned all about nourishing life."[11]

—CHAPTER 3

12 When the spirit moves, we have to have basic skills, which require training, but there are no specific techniques that could be described and taught. While some practical instruction is necessary, it is most important to let our inner faculties come to the fore, and the best way of doing that is to make sure our vital energy is intact and the venues of spirit are open.

13 One way of doing that is to go on retreat, to meditate and release the sensory and conscious mind in favor of the spirit. This process, here described as "fasting" and analogous to the "fasting of the mind" outlined earlier, entails a reversal of ordinary states of perception. We leave the sensory world behind and undertake exercises of concentration and detached observation, opening ourselves to the otherworld—the world of emptiness and Tao in the Chuang-tzu, the world of the ancestors in Confucian ritual.

To connect to ancestors, as outlined in the *Li-chi* (*Liji*; Book of Rites), the sacrificer thinks about the deceased and remembers what they looked like, how they sighed, and how they laughed. He recalls those things that pleased the departed and becomes involved in their emotional life, thus leaving himself as a separate individual behind and establishing an intimate connection to them.

Quite similarly, Taoist "fasting" guides the practitioner to let go of all material benefits (fame and money) as well as all personal evaluations (praise and blame) to reach a state of oblivion and merging with Tao. In both cases, occlusion, sensory deprivation, isolation, and starvation allow entry into things otherwise beyond the senses, opening a sphere outside of ordinary perception. From here, then, the spirit can take over and our natural skills can find practical realization in the world.

Woodworker Ch'ing (Qing) once made a bell-stand from a piece of wood. All who saw it after completion were amazed at the divine quality of the workmanship. The Marquis of Lu went to look at it and asked the carver, "What techniques did you use to make this?"

"I am just a simple artisan, what great techniques would I have? Still, there is one thing. Whenever I get ready to make a bell-stand, I make sure not to diminish my *ch'i* in any way. So I always fast in order to still my mind.[12]

"When I have fasted for three days, I am no longer concerned with congratulations and awards, positions and monetary benefits. When I have fasted for five days, I am no longer concerned with praise or blame, skill or clumsiness. When I have fasted for seven days, I am totally oblivious of my four limbs and body. At this point, there is no more lord or public for me. My skill is fully concentrated and all outside distractions dissolve.

"Only when I get to this point do I go into the forest and examine the trees in their essential nature. If I find one of perfect form and can see a bell-stand in it, I take my hands to it. If not, that's that. I just match heaven with heaven, making the object with my concentrated spirit. That is all."[13]

—CHAPTER 19

14 However good we are at something, though, if it is part of our natural skills (like being at home in the water), we may be able to teach
some basic techniques (like swimming) to anyone, but ultimately the
real knack cannot be learned or taught.

Whatever comes naturally to us is beyond the realm of sensory
transmission, of verbalization, of theoretical or analytical presentation.
How exactly is it that the prodigy plays the piano? We can all learn
about scales and sheet music and hand-tone coordination, but we will
never be quite as good or quite as natural at it.

Along the same lines, the wisdom of the sages is just crummy leftovers; history has only so many lessons. We can study, we can learn,
we can think about it, but we cannot live it. In other words, it is best to
find our personal truth and stay in the present moment.

Once Duke Huan was reading a book in his hall, while Wheelmaker P'ien was making a wheel in the courtyard. Setting his hammer and chisel aside, P'ien went up to the Duke.

"May I ask what you are reading?"

"The words of the sages."

"And those sages are still around?"

"No, they have already died."

"So all you're reading are just the crummy leftovers of men of old."

"How dare you, a simple wheelmaker, criticize my reading? Explain yourself and live; fail to explain and die!"

"Well, I am looking at it from my perspective. When I chisel a wheel and work slowly and gently, there is no firmness; when I work quickly and sharply, there is no aim. Neither slowly nor quickly, that's when I get the right rhythm in my hands and can move along with my mind.

"I can't really express it, but there is a knack to it somehow. I can't teach it to my son, and my son can't learn it from me. For this reason, I am still chiseling wheels at seventy.

"Now, those men of old are dead and they couldn't transmit their knack either. So whatever you are reading is nothing but the crummy leftovers of men of old!"[14]

—CHAPTER 13

1 As we live in the world and try to maintain integrity and fulfill our inborn potential, the question inevitably arises how we should deal with social reality, job offers, and potential promotions. Chuang-tzu in this story is approached by royal messengers of the state he lives in and is offered a position as counselor at court. Should he accept? Should he say no? How much good would his wisdom do if spread in an official government setting? Is service to the world important enough to warrant compromising personal integrity?

2 For Chuang-tzu, the answer to the job offer is clearly negative. The position to him is a form of death, a fossilization. However beautiful, wealthy, and prestigious the setting, it will just lead to a stifling of his natural impulses, limit the unfolding of his true potential, destroy his peace of mind, and lead to life in a straitjacket.

His preference is to be fully alive, to do simple things that may not carry great fame or prestige or income, but are completely satisfying. For him, it is important to be fully involved in what he does, to completely fulfill his nature—just as it is the nature of the turtle to drag its tail through the mud.

The question next is: what is *your* personal mud?

13 □ In the World

Chuang-tzu was fishing in the P'u River, when two messengers from the king of Ch'u approached him. "Our king would like to invite you to serve in the affairs of state."[1]

Chuang-tzu held on to his rod and didn't look around.

"I have heard," he said, "that the state of Ch'u has a sacred turtle, which has been dead for three thousand years. The king has it wrapped in cloth, placed in an ornate box, and keeps it in his ancestral temple.

"Now, let me ask you about his turtle: Would it rather be dead and have its remaining bones be venerated? Or would it rather be alive and drag its tail in the mud?"

"It would rather be alive and drag its tail in the mud."

"Go away. I will continue to drag my tail in the mud."[2]

—CHAPTER 17

3 The state of Lu is in modern Shandong, which is a peninsula jutting into the Eastern Sea and surrounded by the ocean on three sides. However, its capital Ji'nan is inland and quite a ways from the ocean, so the landing of a seabird is a special omen and becomes the reason for a festival.

However, the duke celebrates the bird in the way that he would celebrate a human hero, with a spectacle of fancy music and court dancing, and a great feast with lots of meat and wine. None of this has any appeal to the bird, which is completely out of its element. It refuses the food and dies.

4 Certain things are right for certain beings—for different species and also for different people. What is a delight to one is a horror to another, and there is nothing much we can do to change that. On the other hand, this means that we need to find the right thing that will nourish our own self, even if what we do would be dreadful to another—and by the same token allow others to pursue happiness in their own way. A simple example is that we would not like to eat the dead mouse our cat brings in or the dry seeds the birds like, while they would not enjoy surfing the Internet.

5 There is no real equality among the different creatures or even people in the world, no uniformity and no sameness. There is no point holding people to the same standard. One person easily masters something another may never learn. The point raises important questions about the usefulness of tests, aptitude evaluations, psychological profiles, and the like. How much can the various examinations really tell us about who is good at what?

Once we accept that people and their abilities are unique, we need a language that allows us to express that uniqueness, to create a proper terminology for special expertise and individuality. Language in its turn will create a mental template that allows uniqueness to flourish fully.

Once upon a time, a seabird came to roost in the outskirts of the Lu capital. The duke himself went to see it captured and had it brought to his ancestral temple. He proceeded to provide spectacular entertainment for it with nine-tone music and a full-scale banquet. The bird, however, was dazed and depressed; it did not take one morsel of food or one cup of drink. Three days later it was dead.[3]

This is because the duke nourished the bird with what would be good for himself and not with what would be good for birds. What would be good for birds is to let them perch in the deep forest, fly over shores and dry land, float on rivers and lakes, feed on eels and minnows; to let them follow their flock and rest, find their right place and stay.

Hearing only people's voices was awful for the bird, and what did it care for all the hubbub and excitement? Enchanting nine-tone music, if performed in the wilds around Lake Tung-t'ing (Dongting), would just cause the birds to fly off, the animals to run away, and the fish to dive deep. It is only people who would be attracted, gather round, and enjoy the performance.

When fish are under water, they live; when people are under water, they die. Being fundamentally different in nature, they also like and dislike different things.[4] For this reason, the sages of old never expected uniformity in ability or sameness in activity among different beings. Their names matched reality; their righteousness was a perfect fit. This is called universal mastery and the height of good fortune.[5]

—CHAPTER 18

6 This story contrasts two disciples of Confucius: one known for his indifference to poverty who lives in a hovel that is just about falling down around him, the other famous for his wealth and fastidiousness. One day the latter comes to visit, riding in an ornate carriage, decked out in gorgeous clothes, and equipped with top-notch accessories. He is scandalized.

7 The word used for "wrong" here is *ping* (*bing*), which refers to being sick, ailing, or in distress. The point is that poverty is not a form of disease or distress. Living in the world and realizing our true nature and perfecting our inborn skills may mean being poor, but there is nothing inherently wrong with that. Rather, we should make a clear distinction between outside circumstances and inner realization.

The story echoes an earlier passage when the master was singing a strange song about who made him poor: father, mother, gods, spirits. He came to the conclusion that none of these entities was responsible. Being poor just happened to be his fate.

In other words, we can be comfortable in simple material circumstances and not have anything wrong with us at all. The same also holds true for wealth—even a surplus of money should not change who we are at our most essential core.

8 Most people, however, do things for ulterior motives—to impress their peers, to move in the right circles, to win in competitions, to show off, or to create a flamboyant image in the world. This only leads away from true satisfaction, which is found by doing things just for the sake of doing them, in living our best life and engaging in the activities we do best. The poor disciple, who at first glance is worse off, thus turns out to be the wiser man.

Yüan-hsien lived in Lu, in a shack that just about had walls and was thatched with new grass. It had a door of brushwood that wouldn't close, hanging from a mulberry stick as a doorpost, and bottomless ollas for windows. The two rooms were separated by a rough cloth; water leaked in from above and made the floor damp below. Nonetheless, Yüan-hsien sat proudly, strung his zither, and sang.

In contrast, Tzu-kung usually rode a big horse and dressed in fancy robes of violet and plain silk. One day he came to visit, his carriage too big to even enter the lane to Yüan-hsien's hovel. Yüan-hsien, in a flower cap and barely patched slippers, leaning on a pear cane, greeted him at the gate.[6]

Tzu-kung said, "Oh my! Whatever is wrong with you?"

"From what I have heard, having no possessions is called being poor. Studying and not practicing is called something is wrong. I may be poor, but there is certainly nothing wrong with me!"[7]

Tzu-kung flinched and stepped back, blushing with shame.

Yüan-hsien laughed: "To engage in activities to impress the world, to make friends to establish a 'circle,' to study to be better than others, to teach to show myself off, to use benevolence and righteousness as a cover for all sorts of things, and to deck myself out with carriages and horses—I could never do that!"[8]

—CHAPTER 28

9 The word for "job" (*shih*) literally means "to serve." The idea is that, since Yen Hui is literate, he can obtain a minor position as a scribe or an administrator in the local government.

10 The measurements given in the text are fifty and ten *mou*, respectively. One acre equals six *mou*. Fifty *mou* is enough to feed four people.

The fields are at different distances from the city center. Chinese cities in the old days consisted of large compounds with several one-story buildings, gardens, and stables and thus included places to plant vegetables and keep chickens. Beyond the houses, each city had a ring of farmland including fruit and mulberry trees (for silkworms). This ring was still within the city walls—here described as being "nearby." Larger fields for grain cultivation and rice paddies that needed extensive irrigation were located "outside the city wall."

11 The key concept here is knowing when it is enough (*chih-tsu/zhizu*). It implies a fundamental shift in attitude from deficiency to sufficiency. As Lynne Twist outlines in *The Soul of Money*, it is essential for universal prosperity and happiness that we replace toxic myths that limit possibilities with a new vision: from deficiency thinking (that there is not enough) to a perception of overall sufficiency (that there is plenty to go around).

A key factor to realize sufficiency is to know when it is enough, coupled closely with finding riches in nonmaterial things. It has been shown in many studies by now that the idea of "more is better" is faulty. A certain level of material comfort is needed: when basic needs are met and there is some left over to save and have fun. But there happiness peaks, and more is not better.

Every individual can contribute to a saner and happier world: know when it is enough and stop trying to get more of what you don't need!

Confucius said to Yen Hui, "Oh, come on, Hui. Your family is poor and your house is dilapidated. Why don't you get a job?"[9]

"I don't want a job. I have eight acres of fields outside the city wall, enough for vegetables and grain. I also have an acre and a half of farmland nearby, which gives me enough silk and hemp.[10] Strumming my zithers is enough to give me pleasure; studying Tao with you is enough to make me happy. I don't want a job."[11]

—CHAPTER 28

12 As in ancient Greece, where philosophers were honored, so "men of Tao" were highly esteemed in ancient China. They were people known for their integrity and high level of learning: scholars, poets, philosophers, artists, religious experts, and the like.

As with the traditional feudal courts of Europe and through grant agencies today, such people of renown would be sponsored. In China, their supporters were aristocrats, local rulers, and the imperial court. It was, however—again as in Europe and today—not a one-way system; the local philosopher, wizard, or Taoist also served to enhance the prestige of the sponsor and often aided in legitimation, helping the lord to look good in the eyes of people and his fellow rulers.

13 Lieh-tzu knows that any entanglement with officialdom can backfire. Although he is in dire straits, he does not accept anything that might create bondages and have possible repercussions.

For him, despite his hardship, his personal integrity is of greater significance, and his personal freedom is more important. And when rebellion breaks out and the prince is killed, he cannot be linked with him and suffer his fate.

Lieh-tzu was so poor that he started to look like he was going to starve. A visitor saw him and went to the Prince of Cheng. "Lieh Yü-k'ou (Lie Yukou) is known as a man of Tao. He lives in your state and is in dire poverty! You don't seem to be doing anything about it—don't you cherish men of Tao?"**12**

The prince immediately ordered his officials to send Lieh-tzu some grain. Lieh-tzu saw the messenger at the door, bowed twice, and refused.

The messenger left, and Lieh-tzu stepped back inside. His wife confronted him, beating her breast. She said, "I have heard that the wife and children of men of Tao all find peace and happiness—but here we look like we are going to starve! Now the lord himself takes the trouble to send food and you don't accept it. Certainly that's not destiny!"

Lieh-tzu laughed. "The lord has no clue who I am. He sent the grain on the basis of somebody's say-so. It may well happen that he takes it into his mind to punish me—also on somebody's say-so. For this reason I wouldn't accept it."

In the end, the people rose in rebellion and killed the prince.**13**

—CHAPTER 28

14 As another Chuang-tzu passage states, "In a state of cosmic peace and inner stability, a person emits a heavenly light" (chapter 6). This is the bright light of the spirit within, the "light of inner vision" that forms part of inherent potency and manifests itself as a tendency toward goodness. Spirit as the agent active in human potency is the force of light, which in turn is visible pure *ch'i*. The personal light of inner vision, moreover, is the same as the light of the cosmos. As both participate in one another, they become stronger as they shine forth more harmoniously.

This shining light, moreover, is a kind of charisma. It creates a connection to people and attracts them, making complete strangers approach in the hope to be able to do things with and for such a radiant person. They disregard social convention in favor of this spirited person, in due course entangling him or her in their own visions. It is somewhat like a starstruck fan who follows his idol around, tries to be near him, and imitates him ceaselessly.

15 The higher and more powerful the person such a radiant master encounters, the greater the responsibility he will get. The more responsibility he has, the greater the danger of failure and also of being distracted from the more satisfying endeavors of life. However, if you have that kind of inner light and let it shine outward, you won't be able to get away from it. You may avoid high rank and political involvement, but people will still seek you out—as shown by the piles of shoes outside Lieh-tzu's door.

Lieh-tzu was going to Ch'i but turned back when only halfway. On his way he met Uncle Chaos.

"Why did you turn back?"

"I was scared."

"What made you scared?"

"I ate at ten soup stalls, and at five they served me first!"

"Oh, that's all? Why would that make you scared?"

"If inner sincerity is not dissolved, it is emitted from the body as a sort of radiance. This impacts the minds of others and makes them favor you in disregard of rank and old age. It soon becomes a source of affliction.[14]

"The market people just trade in ready-to-eat soup, they don't make a lot of extra cash. Their profits are slim; their influence is minimal—and yet they treat me special like this. How much more so when it comes to the ruler of a state of ten thousand chariots? His body exhausted from running the state, his mind drained from taking care of administration, he would want me to take things over and make a success of them. This is what made me scared."

"Very good, this perspective you have," Uncle Chaos said. "But even if you stay put, people will still seek you out!"

Not long after, he went to see Lieh-tzu. Outside his door were piles of shoes.[15]

—CHAPTER 32

16 By the same token, if you need to hire someone to do things for you, check her out carefully to see that she has the right qualities. Again, there is no single test or standard for all, but there are some general guidelines on what to look for.

Chuang-tzu in particular looks for qualities such as loyalty, respect, expertise, management skills, reliability, kindness, resourcefulness, clearheadedness, and self-control. Those are all good qualities in assistants and employees, qualities that may make the difference between success and failure. They are also qualities that should be praised and encouraged generally, making the population as a whole more resourceful and reliable.

17 The passage contrasts the behavior of two people receiving important appointments. The first bows deeper each time—from the neck, the chest, and the waist—becoming more humble with increased responsibility. He tries to hide his light and stays close to the wall, trying to be inconspicuous and withdrawing, using his light to the best benefit of all and not for his own self-aggrandizement.

18 In contrast, the second character—the more typical, ordinary person—gets more arrogant and self-important with each higher rank. He draws himself up fully, dances in public, and abandons the formal forms of address required in proper family relations. Each time he takes up more space, lets his radiance escape more widely, makes enemies, and creates disturbances. The position does not do him a great deal of good, and he is probably not even very good at it.

The bottom line: see official positions and responsible jobs as a burden that you may or may not be up to carrying, but don't use them to grow beyond yourself and your social station.

People at the top, when seeing to employ someone, will send him on a distant mission to examine his loyalty and keep him in close proximity to examine his respect. They will make him deal with trouble to examine his management skills and ask his advice unexpectedly to examine his expertise. They will give him a tight deadline to examine his reliability, hand him some donation money to examine his kindness, and tell him about a dangerous situation to examine his resourcefulness. They will also get him to drink heavily to examine his clearheadedness and set him up in mixed company to examine his self-control. By using these nine tests, the unworthy employee is easily found.[16]

When Father Proper got his first position, he bowed from his neck. At his second position, he bowed from his chest. At his third position, he bowed from his waist, stayed in the shadows, and never walked far from the wall. What a model![17]

When an ordinary person gets his first position, he squares his backbone. At his second position, he dances on top of his carriage. At his third position, he calls his uncles by their first names. What a difference![18]

—Chapter 32

1 The sage in a position of power would be sure to create an environment perfectly conducive to people's self-realization in alignment with their personal endowments and specific situations. He would help them eliminate "mental negativity," literally the "thieves" of spirit and *ch'i*, which are the strong reactions to the senses, the emotions—in later texts also called the "six thieves." He would also support them in finding ways to activate their unique qualities, a notion that relates to the idea of aloneness in the attainment of oblivion—the idea that, although part of the greater universe and embedded in social structures, we are all ultimately singular, unique, and alone in ourselves. But realizing this and doing things naturally we can all unfold our particular spontaneous abilities and behaviors in accordance with our inner abilities and tendencies—never quite knowing why and without any need to analyze them.

2 Being in his own completion of aloneness, the sage as ruler would never need to look up to previous sages (like Yao and Shun)—who are long dead and from whom only crummy leftovers remain—or down on the people. The literal expression here is "treat them like older or younger brothers"—in other words, have a specific relationship. Aloneness means overcoming this need for formalized relations.

Rather, the sage is mystically unified with Tao and boundless, an expression that literally combines the words for "darkly immersed" and "fortunate." It expresses a watery expanse and by extension indicates a mind in mystical union with the greater cosmos.

At one with inherent potency, with the power of Tao, the sage has only one desire: to relax in natural so-being. And despite the lack of all conscious planning and effort, just by being himself, the sage affects the world and helps all beings in their own self-realization.

14 □ When in Power

If a great sage were to govern the world, he would let people's minds be easy and open, to have them create their own teachings and change their customs as needed. He would support them in eliminating all mental negativity and help them progress in realizing their unique ambitions. They would come to do things naturally in accordance with their essential nature, never knowing why or wherefore.[1]

Doing things like this, would he ever look up to the teachings of Yao and Shun or, the people being mystically unified and boundless, look down upon them? No. He would only want to be at one with inherent potency and relax his mind there.[2]

—Chapter 12

3 Yao was one of the most venerated sage rulers of antiquity; Hsü Yu was his favored advisor, known as a very wise person. However, in this story, Hsü Yu is trying to escape from his ruler, because the latter is taking the effects of rulership too seriously. As a result people will not take the leader seriously in this generation, which will lead to a moral decline over several generations until the culture sinks into savagery and vandalism. Just as the sage by not trying to govern heals the world, so the ruler by being too serious about governing precipitates its decline.

4 This outlines basic rules of dealing with subjects or subordinates: take care of them and praise them, and they will follow you and do their best to please you; behave in a way they dislike, and off they go.

Politicians have a tendency to pretend, to use sham virtue. They claim to do the best for the common good, yet in fact only disguise their unlimited greed and work massive exploitation on the people for their own profit. Their motivation is usually not sincere, and all their words of good intention just hide the predatory attitude of a raptor.

5 Government should include the perspectives of many, not just a single agency or person making all the decisions. This leads to errors on many levels. Typically those in power are so far removed from the real life of the people that they have no idea what goes on in the world. Led into error, never really connecting to their subjects, they easily make decisions that ruin entire countries. Modern examples abound—leading to environmental disasters, widespread famines, or the massive destruction of infrastructure.

Ni Chüeh (Ni Jue) once met Hsü Yu (Xu You) on the road. He asked: "Where are you going?"

"I am getting away from Yao."

"What do you mean?"

"Yao is so seriously benevolent as if he were raising a family. I am afraid he will be laughed at now, and future generations will deteriorate into cannibalism.[3]

"Now it is not difficult to hold the people together. Love them, and they adore you; benefit them, and they come to you; praise them, and they work hard to please you; do something they detest, and they leave you.

"Both love and benefit come from an attitude of benevolence and righteousness. Only few manage to go easy on these virtues, while lots of people use them to their own advantage. Once they do this, they practice benevolence and righteousness without any real sincerity, faking them when they are in fact mere instruments of raptor-like greed.[4]

"Also, one single person making all the decisions that supposedly benefit the whole world is like having only one brief glimpse of a huge panorama. Yao knows that the wise benefit the world, but he has no idea that they can also ruin it. You only realize that when you get away from the wise."[5]

—CHAPTER 24

6   The ruler here has goals that sound good at first glance but will lead to error and hypocrisy. His goals may be noble, but by creating a conscious effort to do good, he will invite evil, leading to a situation where morals become hypocritical and his ventures will suffer defeat.

As soon as there is a viable model, someone will try to copy it. All success includes defeat on some level. And every change, especially consciously engineered change, always has some unwanted side effects—marginalizing certain groups and creating discord among those who do not benefit from it. Take any administered change in the tax laws, education, health care, or corporate organization—there are always negative side effects and people who do not benefit.

7   The alternative is a soft-footed approach, where change comes as the result of natural unfolding. To work with that, be soft and kind, avoid having guards and patrols, and let go of the military and all kinds of fancy schemes.

Creating a strong military means putting a force into play that may become obstructive. Using artifice, schemes, or force—by lying, cheating, secret plots, and violence—will always backfire. By the same token, going to war in any form is inviting defeat or at least a huge loss of face. Always motivated by egotistic desires, it never pays. One side may technically win, yet even then the price is high, and the militant action will inevitably do more harm than good.

8   The best policy for a ruler is to become selfless and relaxed, matching the inherent purity or integrity of the cosmos: let go of all plans, concerns, schemes, and worries. Then the people are naturally happy and live long. There is no need to do anything further, no need to actively arm or disarm anyone, no need for consciously planned and engineered change.

Duke Wu said to Hsü Wu-kuei, "I've been wanting to talk to you for quite some time. I want to love the people, act in righteousness, and disarm the country—is that doable?"

"No, it's not. Loving the people is the first step in harming them. Acting in righteousness and disarming the country are the root of increased warfare. If you do this, my guess is you will fail. Usually efforts to do good become instruments of evil. While you may act in benevolence and righteousness, your action will soon turn into hypocrisy. Just as models always produce copies, in success there is always defeat; change always leads to marginalization and discord.**6**

"On the other hand, you should also avoid having large numbers of guards in your palace courtyards or mounted patrols around your halls. Never amass troops that might obstruct your interests, and by all means do not even try to overcome others with artifice, schemes, or force. Killing the people of another state and taking over its territory may satisfy your selfish desires and pay tribute to your egotistic spirit. But who in this battle would be in the right? Who would be the victor?**7**

"Now, better give up all selfishness and cultivate sincerity in your breast; naturally match the integrity of heaven and earth and let go of all worries. This will let the people escape from death naturally—so what need would you have to disarm the country?"**8**

—Chapter 24

9　One way of reaching the state of mind necessary to let things go even when you have the power to make changes is to get personally involved. There is a healthy sort of selfishness in that self-preservation and a good life should take precedence over material possessions and political power. In this story, the loss of a limb and the impact of worry on the mind are contrasted with the gain of a piece of territory.

There is, when it comes down to it, no contest. Once everything is put in its proper perspective, no land, resource, or influence is worth the trouble it causes in terms of loss of life, suffering, and social disruption. The more personally—in their own bodies and families—politicians are involved in the decisions they make, the less damage those decisions are likely to cause.

The states of Han and Wei were fighting over a piece of conquered territory. Hua-tzu (Huazi) went to see Duke Chao-hsi (Zhaoxi), the ruler of Han. He looked depressed.

Hua-tzu said, "Let's assume the world writes up an agreement and puts it before you. Its text reads: 'If you take this with your left hand, your right hand will be chopped off. If you take it with your right hand, your left hand will be chopped off. But if you take it, you will get the world.' Would you take it?"

"I certainly would not."

"Great. Look at it this way then: your two arms are more important to you than the world. Your body is even more important than your arms. In addition, the state of Han is far less significant than the whole world, and this piece of land you're fighting over today is even less significant than the state of Han. You see, it is totally unacceptable to harm your body and labor your life by being depressed and worrying over a mere piece of land!"[9]

—CHAPTER 28

10 There are also some passages that tell stories not about rulers but about people serving in office and the effect it has on their lives.

Tseng-tzu, one of Confucius's disciples, is known as a paragon of filial piety who does everything for his parents. At first his salary is small, but he has good family relations: he is happy and contented. Later his salary is very large, but his parents have died and he has no one to share his wealth with; he is sad and depressed. The upshot is that relationships are more important than money, that happiness depends to a certain degree on material security, but once that is guaranteed, it is a matter of nonmaterial aspects.

As for the salary he received, officials in ancient China were paid annually in grain. One goblet (*fu*) is 6 pecks (*tou*), 4 pints (*sheng*), which comes to about 11.5 gallons or 45 liters in modern measurements. One bucket (*chung*) is 4 pecks, which equals 7 gallons or 28 liters. In other words, Tseng-tzu first made 34.5 gallons of grain, in contrast to 21,000 gallons in his second appointment—quite a difference.

11 "Hang-up" translates *hsüan* (*xuan*), which quite literally means "to hang up"—a less colloquial translation is "entanglements." The term refers to his involvement with and connections to the world. The question here is whether being a filial person unable to enjoy his large salary, he was free from worldly entanglements. The answer is no, he wasn't, since filial piety in itself creates connections and thus involvement and emotions. Being truly free means allowing things to come and go and not reacting to them.

Tseng-tzu (Zengzi) served twice in office, with a different attitude each time. He said, "The first time I served, I was taking care of my parents. I only received three goblets of grain but was happy in my heart. The next time I served, I made three thousand buckets but I could not share it with my parents and was sad in my heart."[10]

Another disciple asked Confucius about him: "Does this mean that Tseng-tzu was free from hang-ups?"

"But he was totally hung up! If he had had no hang-ups, why all that sadness? He would have glanced at his three goblets and three thousand buckets no more than at so many sparrows or bugs passing by."[11]

—CHAPTER 27

12 Here is a case of someone without hang-ups, who can take or leave positions and income as they arrive. His breath is calm and subtle, which means that his mind is calm and relaxed, kept under control. Mind and breath are intimately related, the breath in many ways the outward signal of the current state of mind.

For example, watching a scary movie, people hold their breath. Engaged in passionate embrace, they pant with excitement. At times of fear, tension, worry, sorrow, or stress, breathing becomes tight, shallow, and rapid. On the other hand, when we lie down to relax or sleep, we breathe deeply and slowly. Breathing is therefore an obvious and easily accessible tool for calming the mind, opening a state of relaxation, and allowing the inward turning of attention.

13 Here the distinction is made between personal merit and the arrival of positions or fame. Gain and loss are not things we can control; they are impersonal events dictated by fate, destiny, circumstances beyond our control. As a result, they are best viewed with detachment, using a distant observer or witness consciousness, a mental position of distanced seeing, a faculty of taking a step back from involvement with experiences and emotions. The detached observer is something all people have at times, such as the ability to laugh at themselves when in a strange situation or the faculty to take a step back and examine circumstances from a distance.

It also helps to question where the honor, the fame, the value is in this case. If it is in the position, then my filling it is coincidental, and I just have to do the best I can to match it. If it is in me, then wherever I am I have just the same amount of honor and self-worth, and I can give my best to the position I happen to be in without getting attached to it.

14 Beyond all these considerations and activities, it is in the end much more important to have a relaxed life and enjoy what you love to do than to worry about what others think. Take a leisurely walk, go for a swim, enjoy a game of sports, play with the kids, engage in a hobby, have dinner with friends, even work—whatever gives maximum pleasure and fulfills you most!

Ch'ien Wu (Qian Wu) asked Sunshu Ao, "Three times you served as senior magistrate and did not luxuriate in splendor. Three times you were dismissed and did not look depressed. First I doubted that this was for real, but now I see your breath is calm and subtle. Do you have some special method of controlling your mind?"[12]

"How would I be special beyond other people? All I do is understand that when a position comes to me, I can't prevent it; when it goes away, I can't stop it. Thinking of all gain and loss as impersonal events, I have no cause for depression. That is all. So how am I special beyond others?

"Also, I have no clue whether the honor resides in the position or in myself. If it is in the position, I have nothing to do with it; if it is in myself, the position is irrelevant.[13]

"And now, my friend, I am going to take a leisurely walk, looking round in all directions. I really have no time to worry whether people honor or despise me."[14]

—CHAPTER 21

15 Last, but certainly not least, there is a story about someone who is in office but wishes to retire or at least get away from it all. Prince Mou was known as trying to live the life of a hermit and attain Tao but could not leave the burdens of his rulership behind.

This is a common problem today, when people try to get away, going on vacation or staying at home or visiting friends, but always take work with them. Today this is made easier by all sorts of technological gadgets, so that we remain connected at all times and have both leisure and work with us—but do we give 100 percent to either?

16 Prince Mou—like modern executives—understands very well that the key to getting away and relaxing is to place a higher importance on life and health than on success and money. But, again like many people today, he has no control over his mind and keeps thinking and worrying about his work.

17 If you are not able to control your thoughts, it is best to do what you feel like doing, even if it means leaving work early or taking work to the beach. Having no control over urges and suppressing your desires create a double whammy. The spirit is burdened and labored, the body is increasingly exhausted, and a heart attack follows—not the best way to reach extended longevity.

So, whether in office and under pressure or on vacation and at leisure, you can still try to find what is most pleasing and brings peace to body and mind in the present moment—abstaining from value judgments and never beating yourself up over one thing or another.

Prince Mou of Wei was in the Central Mountains. He said to the sage Chan-tzu (Zhanzi), "My body is here among rivers and seas, but my mind is still back in the Wei palace. What can I do?"**15**

"Value life above everything. Once you value life highly, all profit and gain will seem negligible."

"I realize that. But I have no control over myself."**16**

"If you have no control over yourself, then just do what you like!"

"Won't my spirit hate that?"

"Having no control over yourself and forcing yourself to not do what you really like creates a double burden on the spirit. People who harm themselves this way never achieve any form of long life."**17**

Ruling a state of ten thousand chariots, Mou had a much harder time to retire among the cliffs and caverns than an ordinary official. He did not actually reach Tao, but he certainly can be said to have had that intention.

—CHAPTER 28

Suggestions for Further Reading

Previous Translations

Graham, A. C., trans. *Chuang-tzu: The Inner Chapters.* 1981. Indianapolis: Hackett, 2001.

Hamill, Sam, and Jerome P. Seaton, trans. *The Essential Chuang Tzu.* Boston: Shambhala, 1998.

Hinton, David, trans. *Chuang Tzu: The Inner Chapters.* Washington, DC: Counterpoint, 1997.

Höchsmann, Hyun, and Guorong Yang, trans. *Zhuangzi.* New York: Pearson Longman, 2007.

Legge, James, trans. *The Sacred Books of China: The Texts of Taoism.* 1895. New York: Dover, 1962.

Mair, Victor H., trans. *Wandering on the Way: Early Taoist Tales and Parables of Chuang Tzu.* New York: Bantam, 1994.

Palmer, Martin, et al., trans. *The Book of Chuang Tzu.* 1996. New York: Penguin, 2006.

Watson, Burton, trans. *The Complete Works of Chuang-tzu.* New York: Columbia University Press, 1968.

Ziporyn, Brook, trans. *Zhuangzi: The Essential Writings with Selections from Traditional Commentaries.* Indianapolis: Hackett, 2009.

Chuang-tzu Studies

Allinson, Robert E. *Chuang-Tzu for Spiritual Transformation: An Analysis of the Inner Chapters.* Albany: State University of New York Press, 1989.

Ames, Roger T., ed. *Wandering at Ease in the Zhuangzi.* Albany: State University of New York Press, 1998.

Chang, Chung-yüan. "The Philosophy of Taoism According to Chuang-tzu." *Philosophy East and West* 27, no. 4 (1977): 409–22.

Coutinho, Steve. *Chuang-tzu and Early Chinese Philosophy: Vagueness, Transformation, and Paradox.* Burlington, VT: Ashgate, 2004.

Girardot, Norman. *Myth and Meaning in Early Daoism: The Theme of Chaos (Hundun)*. 1983. Dunedin, FL: Three Pines Press, 2009.

Graham, A. C. *Studies in Chinese Philosophy and Philosophical Literature*. Albany: State University of New York Press, 1990.

Kjellberg, Paul, and Philip J. Ivanhoe, eds. *Essays on Skepticism, Relativism, and Ethics in the Zhuangzi*. Albany: State University of New York Press, 1996.

Liu, Xiaogan. *Classifying the Zhuangzi Chapters*. Michigan Monographs in Chinese Studies, no. 65. Ann Arbor: University of Michigan / Center for Chinese Studies, 1994.

Mair, Victor H., ed. *Experimental Essays on Zhuangzi*. 1983. Dunedin, FL: Three Pines Press, 2010.

Merton, Thomas. *The Way of Chuang Tzu*. 2nd ed. New York: New Directions, 2010.

Roth, Harold D. *A Companion to Angus C. Graham's Chuang Tzu: The Inner Chapters*. Honolulu: University of Hawai'i Press, 2003.

Tsai, Chih-chung. *Zhuangzi Speaks: The Music of Nature*. Translated by Brian Bruya. Princeton, NJ: Princeton University Press, 1992.

Waltham, Clae. *Chuang Tzu: Genius of the Absurd*. New York: Ace Books, 1971.

Wang, Youru. *Linguistic Strategies in Daoist Zhuangzi and Chan Buddhism: The Other Way of Speaking*. New York: Routledge, 2003.

Wu, Chung. *The Wisdom of Zhuang Zi on Daoism*. New York: Peter Lang, 2007.

Wu, Kuang-ming. *The Butterfly as Companion: Meditations on the First Three Chapters of the Chuang Tzu*. Albany: State University of New York Press, 1990.

———. *Chuang Tzu: World Philosopher at Play*. New York: Crossroad / Scholars Press, 1982.

Taoist Dimensions

Blofeld, John. *The Secret and Sublime: Taoist Mysteries and Magic*. New York: Dutton, 1973.

Bokenkamp, Stephen R. *Early Daoist Scriptures*. With a contribution by Peter Nickerson. Berkeley: University of California Press, 1997.

Campany, Robert F. *Making Transcendents: Ascetics and Social Memory in Early Medieval China*. Honolulu: University of Hawai'i Press, 2009.

Cleary, Thomas. *Vitality, Energy, Spirit: A Taoist Sourcebook*. Boston: Shambhala, 1991.

Csikszentmihalyi, Mark. *Readings in Han Chinese Thought*. Indianapolis: Hackett, 2006.

Despeux, Catherine, and Livia Kohn. *Women in Daoism*. Cambridge, MA: Three Pines Press, 2003.

Graham, A. C. *The Book of Lieh-tzu: A Classic of the Tao*. 1960. New York: Columbia University Press, 1990.

Kohn, Livia. *Chinese Healing Exercises: The Tradition of Daoyin*. Honolulu: University of Hawai'i Press, 2008.

———. *Daoism and Chinese Culture*. Cambridge, MA: Three Pines Press, 2001.

———, ed. *Daoist Body Cultivation: Traditional Models and Contemporary Practices*. Magdalena, NM: Three Pines Press, 2006.

———. *Daoist Dietetics: Food for Immortality*. Dunedin, FL: Three Pines Press, 2010.

———. *Early Chinese Mysticism: Philosophy and Soteriology in the Taoist Tradition*. Princeton, NJ: Princeton University Press, 1992.

———. *Health and Long Life: The Chinese Way*. Cambridge, MA: Three Pines Press, 2005.

———. *Monastic Life in Medieval Daoism: A Cross-Cultural Perspective*. Honolulu: University of Hawai'i Press, 2003.

———. *Readings in Chinese Mysticism*. Dunedin, FL: Three Pines Press, 2009.

———. *Sitting in Oblivion: The Heart of Daoist Meditation*. Dunedin, FL: Three Pines Press, 2010.

———, ed. *Taoist Meditation and Longevity Techniques*. Ann Arbor: University of Michigan / Center for Chinese Studies, 1989.

Kohn, Livia, and Michael LaFargue, eds. *Lao-tzu and the Tao-te-ching*. Albany: State University of New York Press, 1998.

Littlejohn, Ronnie. *Daoism: An Introduction*. New York: I. B. Tauris, 2009.

Major, John S., Sarah A. Queen, Andrew S. Meyer, and Harold D. Roth. *The Huainanzi: A Guide to the Theory and Practice of Government in Early Han China*. New York: Columbia University Press, 2010.

Miller, James. *The Way of Highest Clarity: Nature, Vision and Revelation in Medieval Taoism*. Magdalena, NM: Three Pines Press, 2008.

Mollier, Christine. *Buddhism and Taoism Face to Face: Scripture, Ritual, and Iconographic Exchange in Medieval China*. Honolulu: University of Hawai'i Press, 2008.

Pregadio, Fabrizio, ed. *The Encyclopedia of Taoism*. London: Routledge, 2008.

Robinet, Isabelle. *Taoism: Growth of a Religion*. Translated by Phyllis Brooks. Stanford: Stanford University Press, 1997.

Roth, Harold D. *Original Tao: Inward Training and the Foundations of Taoist Mysticism*. New York: Columbia University Press, 1999.

Sakade, Yoshinobu. *Taoism, Medicine, and Qi in China and Japan*. Osaka: Kansai University Press, 2007.

Santee, Robert. *An Integrative Approach to Counseling: Bridging Chinese Thought, Evolutionary Theory, and Stress Management.* New York: Sage, 2007.

Schipper, Kristofer M. *The Taoist Body.* Translated by Karen C. Duval. Berkeley: University of California Press, 1993.

Silvers, Brock. *The Taoist Manual: Applying Taoism to Daily Life.* Honolulu: Sacred Mountain Press, 2005.

Slingerland, Edward. *Effortless Action: Wu-wei as a Conceptual Metaphor and Spiritual Ideal in Ancient China.* New York: Oxford University Press, 2003.

Wong, Eva. *The Shambhala Guide to Taoism.* Boston: Shambhala, 1997.

Other Works Cited

Deikman, Arthur. *The Observing Self: Mysticism and Psychotherapy.* Boston: Beacon Press, 1982.

Ford, Debbie. *The Dark Side of the Light Chasers.* 10th anniv. ed. New York: Riverhead Books, 2010.

Hawkins, David R. *Power vs. Force: The Hidden Determinants of Human Behavior.* Carlsbad, CA: Hay House, 2002.

Jaspers, Karl. *The Origin and Goal of History.* New Haven: Yale University Press, 1953.

Nhat Hanh, Thich. *The Miracle of Mindfulness: A Manual on Meditation.* Rev. ed. Boston: Beacon Press, 1987.

Twist, Lynne. *The Soul of Money: Reclaiming the Wealth of Our Inner Resources.* New York: W. W. Norton, 2006.

Van de Wetering, Janwillem. *The Empty Mirror: Experiences in a Japanese Zen Monastery.* 1973. New York: St. Martin's Griffin, 1999.

Zukav, Gary. *Soul Stories.* New York: Simon & Schuster, 2000.

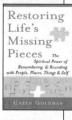

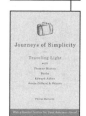

Children's Spirituality

Remembering My Grandparent: A Kid's Own Grief Workbook in the Christian Tradition *by Nechama Liss-Levinson, PhD, and Rev. Molly Phinney Baskette, MDiv* 8 x 10, 48 pp, 2-color text, HC, 978-1-59473-212-6 **$16.99** *For ages 7 & up*

Does God Ever Sleep? *by Joan Sauro, CSJ*
A charming nighttime reminder that God is always present in our lives.
10 x 8½, 32 pp, Full-color photos, Quality PB, 978-1-59473-110-5 **$8.99** *For ages 3–6*

Does God Forgive Me? *by August Gold; Full-color photos by Diane Hardy Waller*
Gently shows how God forgives all that we do if we are truly sorry.
10 x 8½, 32 pp, Full-color photos, Quality PB, 978-1-59473-142-6 **$8.99** *For ages 3–6*

God Said Amen *by Sandy Eisenberg Sasso; Full-color illus. by Avi Katz*
A warm and inspiring tale that shows us that we need only reach out to each other to find the answers to our prayers.
9 x 12, 32 pp, Full-color illus., HC, 978-1-58023-080-3 **$16.95*** *For ages 4 & up*

How Does God Listen? *by Kay Lindahl; Full-color photos by Cynthia Maloney*
How do we know when God is listening to us? Children will find the answers to these questions as they engage their senses while the story unfolds, learning how God listens in the wind, waves, clouds, hot chocolate, perfume, our tears and our laughter.
10 x 8½, 32 pp, Full-color photos, Quality PB, 978-1-59473-084-9 **$8.99** *For ages 3–6*

In God's Hands *by Lawrence Kushner and Gary Schmidt; Full-color illus. by Matthew J. Baek*
9 x 12, 32 pp, Full-color illus., HC, 978-1-58023-224-1 **$16.99*** *For ages 5 & up*

In God's Name *by Sandy Eisenberg Sasso; Full-color illus. by Phoebe Stone*
Like an ancient myth in its poetic text and vibrant illustrations, this award-winning modern fable about the search for God's name celebrates the diversity and, at the same time, the unity of all the people of the world.
9 x 12, 32 pp, Full-color illus., HC, 978-1-879045-26-2 **$16.99*** *For ages 4 & up*

Also available in Spanish: **El nombre de Dios**
9 x 12, 32 pp, Full-color illus., HC, 978-1-893361-63-8 **$16.95**

In Our Image: God's First Creatures
by Nancy Sohn Swartz; Full-color illus. by Melanie Hall
A playful new twist on the Genesis story—from the perspective of the animals. Celebrates the interconnectedness of nature and the harmony of all living things.
9 x 12, 32 pp, Full-color illus., HC, 978-1-879045-99-6 **$16.95*** *For ages 4 & up*

Noah's Wife: The Story of Naamah
by Sandy Eisenberg Sasso; Full-color illus. by Bethanne Andersen
Opens young readers' religious imaginations to new ideas about the well-known story of the Flood. When God tells Noah to bring the animals of the world onto the ark, God also calls on Naamah, Noah's wife, to save each plant on Earth.
9 x 12, 32 pp, Full-color illus., HC, 978-1-58023-134-3 **$16.95*** *For ages 4 & up*

Also available: **Naamah:** Noah's Wife (A Board Book)
by Sandy Eisenberg Sasso; Full-color illus. by Bethanne Andersen
5 x 5, 24 pp, Full-color illus., Board Book, 978-1-893361-56-0 **$7.95** *For ages 0–4*

Where Does God Live? *by August Gold and Matthew J. Perlman*
Helps children and their parents find God in the world around us with simple, practical examples children can relate to.
10 x 8½, 32 pp, Full-color photos, Quality PB, 978-1-893361-39-3 **$8.99** *For ages 3–6*

* A book from Jewish Lights, SkyLight Paths' sister imprint

Children's Spirituality—Board Books

Children's Spiritual Biography

MULTICULTURAL, NONDENOMINATIONAL, NONSECTARIAN

Ten Amazing People
And How They Changed the World
by Maura D. Shaw; Foreword by Dr. Robert Coles
Full-color illus. by Stephen Marchesi

For ages 7 & up

Shows kids that spiritual people can have an exciting impact on the world around them. Kids will delight in reading about these amazing people and what they accomplished through their words and actions.

Black Elk • Dorothy Day • Malcolm X • Mahatma Gandhi • Martin Luther King, Jr. • Mother Teresa • Janusz Korczak • Desmond Tutu • Thich Nhat Hanh • Albert Schweitzer

"Best Juvenile/Young Adult Non-Fiction Book of the Year."
—*Independent Publisher*

"Will inspire adults and children alike."
—*Globe and Mail* (Toronto)

8½ x 11, 48 pp, Full-color illus., HC, 978-1-893361-47-8 **$17.95** *For ages 7 & up*

Spiritual Biographies for Young People
For Ages 7 & Up

By Maura D. Shaw; Illus. by Stephen Marchesi
6¾ x 8¾, 32 pp, Full-color and b/w illus., HC

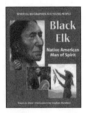
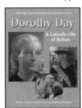
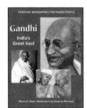
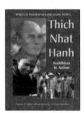

Black Elk: Native American Man of Spirit
Through historically accurate illustrations and photos, inspiring age-appropriate activities and Black Elk's own words, this colorful biography introduces children to a remarkable person who ensured that the traditions and beliefs of his people would not be forgotten.
978-1-59473-043-6 **$12.99**

Dorothy Day: A Catholic Life of Action
Introduces children to one of the most inspiring women of the twentieth century, a down-to-earth spiritual leader who saw the presence of God in every person she met. Includes practical activities, a timeline and a list of important words to know.
978-1-59473-011-5 **$12.99**

Gandhi: India's Great Soul
The only biography of Gandhi that balances a simple text with illustrations, photos and activities that encourage children and adults to talk about how to make changes happen without violence. Introduces children to important concepts of freedom, equality and justice among people of all backgrounds and religions.
978-1-893361-91-1 **$12.95**

Thich Nhat Hanh: Buddhism in Action
Warm illustrations, photos, age-appropriate activities and Thich Nhat Hanh's own poems introduce a great man to children in a way they can understand and enjoy. Includes a list of important Buddhist words to know.
978-1-893361-87-4 **$12.95**

Spiritual Poetry—The Mystic Poets

Experience these mystic poets as you never have before. Each beautiful, compact book includes a brief introduction to the poet's time and place, a summary of the major themes of the poet's mysticism and religious tradition, essential selections from the poet's most important works, and an appreciative preface by a contemporary spiritual writer.

Hafiz
The Mystic Poets
Translated and with Notes by Gertrude Bell
Preface by Ibrahim Gamard
Hafiz is known throughout the world as Persia's greatest poet, with sales of his poems in Iran today only surpassed by those of the Qur'an itself. His probing and joyful verse speaks to people from all backgrounds who long to taste and feel divine love and experience harmony with all living things.
5 x 7¼, 144 pp, HC, 978-1-59473-009-2 **$16.99**

Hopkins
The Mystic Poets
Preface by Rev. Thomas Ryan, CSP
Gerard Manley Hopkins, Christian mystical poet, is beloved for his use of fresh language and startling metaphors to describe the world around him. Although his verse is lovely, beneath the surface lies a searching soul, wrestling with and yearning for God.
5 x 7¼, 112 pp, HC, 978-1-59473-010-8 **$16.99**

Tagore
The Mystic Poets
Preface by Swami Adiswarananda
Rabindranath Tagore is often considered the Shakespeare of modern India. A great mystic, Tagore was the teacher of W. B. Yeats and Robert Frost, the close friend of Albert Einstein and Mahatma Gandhi, and the winner of the Nobel Prize for Literature. This beautiful sampling of Tagore's two most important works, *The Gardener* and *Gitanjali,* offers a glimpse into his spiritual vision that has inspired people around the world.
5 x 7¼, 144 pp, HC, 978-1-59473-008-5 **$16.99**

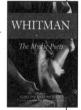

Whitman
The Mystic Poets
Preface by Gary David Comstock
Walt Whitman was the most innovative and influential poet of the nineteenth century. This beautiful sampling of Whitman's most important poetry from *Leaves of Grass,* and selections from his prose writings, offers a glimpse into the spiritual side of his most radical themes—love for country, love for others and love of self.
5 x 7¼, 192 pp, HC, 978-1-59473-041-2 **$16.99**

Spirituality of the Seasons

Autumn: A Spiritual Biography of the Season
Edited by Gary Schmidt and Susan M. Felch; Illus. by Mary Azarian
Rejoice in autumn as a time of preparation and reflection. Includes Wendell Berry, David James Duncan, Robert Frost, A. Bartlett Giamatti, E. B. White, P. D. James, Julian of Norwich, Garret Keizer, Tracy Kidder, Anne Lamott, May Sarton.
6 x 9, 320 pp, b/w illus., Quality PB, 978-1-59473-118-1 **$18.99**

Spring: A Spiritual Biography of the Season
Edited by Gary Schmidt and Susan M. Felch; Illus. by Mary Azarian
Explore the gentle unfurling of spring and reflect on how nature celebrates rebirth and renewal. Includes Jane Kenyon, Lucy Larcom, Harry Thurston, Nathaniel Hawthorne, Noel Perrin, Annie Dillard, Martha Ballard, Barbara Kingsolver, Dorothy Wordsworth, Donald Hall, David Brill, Lionel Basney, Isak Dinesen, Paul Laurence Dunbar. 6 x 9, 352 pp, b/w illus., Quality PB, 978-1-59473-246-1 **$18.99**

Summer: A Spiritual Biography of the Season
Edited by Gary Schmidt and Susan M. Felch; Illus. by Barry Moser
"A sumptuous banquet.... These selections lift up an exquisite wholeness found within an everyday sophistication." — ★ *Publishers Weekly* starred review
Includes Anne Lamott, Luci Shaw, Ray Bradbury, Richard Selzer, Thomas Lynch, Walt Whitman, Carl Sandburg, Sherman Alexie, Madeleine L'Engle, Jamaica Kincaid.
6 x 9, 304 pp, b/w illus., Quality PB, 978-1-59473-183-9 **$18.99**
HC, 978-1-59473-083-2 **$21.99**

Winter: A Spiritual Biography of the Season
Edited by Gary Schmidt and Susan M. Felch; Illus. by Barry Moser
"This outstanding anthology features top-flight nature and spirituality writers on the fierce, inexorable season of winter.... Remarkably lively and warm, despite the icy subject." — ★ *Publishers Weekly* starred review
Includes Will Campbell, Rachel Carson, Annie Dillard, Donald Hall, Ron Hansen, Jane Kenyon, Jamaica Kincaid, Barry Lopez, Kathleen Norris, John Updike, E. B. White.
6 x 9, 288 pp, b/w illus., Deluxe PB w/ flaps, 978-1-893361-92-8 **$18.95**
HC, 978-1-893361-53-9 **$21.95**

Spirituality / Animal Companions

Blessing the Animals: Prayers and Ceremonies to Celebrate God's Creatures, Wild and Tame *Edited and with Introductions by Lynn L. Caruso*
5¼ x 7¼, 256 pp, Quality PB, 978-1-59473-253-9 **$15.99**; HC, 978-1-59473-145-7 **$19.99**

Remembering My Pet: A Kid's Own Spiritual Workbook for When a Pet Dies
by Nechama Liss-Levinson, PhD, and Rev. Molly Phinney Baskette, MDiv; Foreword by Lynn L. Caruso
8 x 10, 48 pp, 2-color text, HC, 978-1-59473-221-8 **$16.99**

What Animals Can Teach Us about Spirituality: Inspiring Lessons from Wild and Tame Creatures *by Diana L. Guerrero* 6 x 9, 176 pp, Quality PB, 978-1-893361-84-3 **$16.95**

Spirituality—A Week Inside

Lighting the Lamp of Wisdom: A Week Inside a Yoga Ashram
by John Ittner; Foreword by Dr. David Frawley
6 x 9, 192 pp, b/w photos, Quality PB, 978-1-893361-52-2 **$15.95**

Making a Heart for God: A Week Inside a Catholic Monastery
by Dianne Aprile; Foreword by Brother Patrick Hart, OCSO
6 x 9, 224 pp, b/w photos, Quality PB, 978-1-893361-49-2 **$16.95**

Waking Up: A Week Inside a Zen Monastery
by Jack Maguire; Foreword by John Daido Loori, Roshi
6 x 9, 224 pp, b/w photos, Quality PB, 978-1-893361-55-3 **$16.95**; HC, 978-1-893361-13-3 **$21.95**

Spirituality

The Heartbeat of God: Finding the Sacred in the Middle of Everything
by Katharine Jefferts Schori; Foreword by Joan Chittister, OSB
Explores our connections to other people, to other nations and with the environment through the lens of faith. 6 x 9, 240 pp, HC, 978-1-59473-292-8 **$21.99**

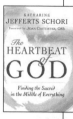

A Dangerous Dozen: Twelve Christians Who Threatened the Status Quo but Taught Us to Live Like Jesus
by the Rev. Canon C. K. Robertson, PhD; Foreword by Archbishop Desmond Tutu
Profiles twelve visionary men and women who challenged society and showed the world a different way of living. 6 x 9, 160 pp (est), Quality PB, 978-1-59473-298-0 **$16.99**

Decision Making & Spiritual Discernment: The Sacred Art of Finding Your Way *by Nancy L. Bieber*
Presents three essential aspects of Spirit-led decision making: willingness, attentiveness and responsiveness. 5½ x 8½, 208 pp, Quality PB, 978-1-59473-289-8 **$16.99**

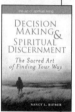

Laugh Your Way to Grace: Reclaiming the Spiritual Power of Humor
by Rev. Susan Sparks A powerful, humorous case for laughter as a spiritual, healing path. 6 x 9, 176 pp, Quality PB, 978-1-59473-280-5 **$16.99**

Living into Hope: A Call to Spiritual Action for Such a Time as This
by Rev. Dr. Joan Brown Campbell; Foreword by Karen Armstrong
A visionary minister speaks out on the pressing issues that face us today, offering inspiration and challenge. 6 x 9, 208 pp, HC, 978-1-59473-283-6 **$21.99**

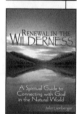

Claiming Earth as Common Ground: The Ecological Crisis through the Lens of Faith
by Andrea Cohen-Kiener; Foreword by Rev. Sally Bingham
6 x 9, 192 pp, Quality PB, 978-1-59473-261-4 **$16.99**

Bread, Body, Spirit: Finding the Sacred in Food
Edited and with Introductions by Alice Peck 6 x 9, 224 pp, Quality PB, 978-1-59473-242-3 **$19.99**

Creating a Spiritual Retirement: A Guide to the Unseen Possibilities in Our Lives
by Molly Srode 6 x 9, 208 pp, b/w photos, Quality PB, 978-1-59473-050-4 **$14.99**

Creative Aging: Rethinking Retirement and Non-Retirement in a Changing World
by Marjory Zoet Bankson 6 x 9, 160 pp, Quality PB, 978-1-59473-281-2 **$16.99**

Keeping Spiritual Balance as We Grow Older: More than 65 Creative Ways to Use Purpose, Prayer, and the Power of Spirit to Build a Meaningful Retirement
by Molly and Bernie Srode 8 x 8, 224 pp, Quality PB, 978-1-59473-042-9 **$16.99**

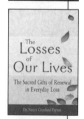

Hearing the Call across Traditions: Readings on Faith and Service
Edited by Adam Davis; Foreword by Eboo Patel
6 x 9, 352 pp, Quality PB, 978-1-59473-303-1 **$18.99**; HC, 978-1-59473-264-5 **$29.99**

Honoring Motherhood: Prayers, Ceremonies & Blessings
Edited and with Introductions by Lynn L. Caruso 5 x 7¼, 272 pp, HC, 978-1-59473-239-3 **$19.99**

Journeys of Simplicity: Traveling Light with Thomas Merton, Bashō, Edward Abbey, Annie Dillard & Others *by Philip Harnden*
5 x 7¼, 144 pp, Quality PB, 978-1-59473-181-5 **$12.99**; 128 pp, HC, 978-1-893361-76-8 **$16.95**

The Losses of Our Lives: The Sacred Gifts of Renewal in Everyday Loss
by Dr. Nancy Copeland-Payton 6 x 9, 192 pp, HC, 978-1-59473-271-3 **$19.99**

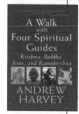

Renewal in the Wilderness: A Spiritual Guide to Connecting with God in the Natural World *by John Lionberger*
6 x 9, 176 pp, b/w photos, Quality PB, 978-1-59473-219-5 **$16.99**

Soul Fire: Accessing Your Creativity
by Thomas Ryan, CSP 6 x 9, 160 pp, Quality PB, 978-1-59473-243-0 **$16.99**

A Spirituality for Brokenness: Discovering Your Deepest Self in Difficult Times
by Terry Taylor 6 x 9, 176 pp, Quality PB, 978-1-59473-229-4 **$16.99**

A Walk with Four Spiritual Guides: Krishna, Buddha, Jesus, and Ramakrishna
by Andrew Harvey 5½ x 8½, 192 pp, b/w photos & illus., Quality PB, 978-1-59473-138-9 **$15.99**

The Workplace and Spirituality: New Perspectives on Research and Practice
Edited by Dr. Joan Marques, Dr. Satinder Dhiman and Dr. Richard King
6 x 9, 256 pp, HC, 978-1-59473-260-7 **$29.99**

Spirituality & Crafts

Beading—The Creative Spirit: Finding Your Sacred Center through the Art of Beadwork *by Rev. Wendy Ellsworth*
Invites you on a spiritual pilgrimage into the kaleidoscope world of glass and color. 7 x 9, 240 pp, 8-page color insert, 40+ b/w photos and 40 diagrams, Quality PB, 978-1-59473-267-6 **$18.99**

Contemplative Crochet: A Hands-On Guide for Interlocking Faith and Craft *by Cindy Crandall-Frazier; Foreword by Linda Skolnik*
Illuminates the spiritual lessons you can learn through crocheting.
7 x 9, 208 pp, b/w photos, Quality PB, 978-1-59473-238-6 **$16.99**

The Knitting Way: A Guide to Spiritual Self-Discovery
by Linda Skolnik and Janice MacDaniels Examines how you can explore and strengthen your spiritual life through knitting.
7 x 9, 240 pp, b/w photos, Quality PB, 978-1-59473-079-5 **$16.99**

The Painting Path: Embodying Spiritual Discovery through Yoga, Brush and Color *by Linda Novick; Foreword by Richard Segalman*
Explores the divine connection you can experience through art.
7 x 9, 208 pp, 8-page color insert, plus b/w photos,
Quality PB, 978-1-59473-226-3 **$18.99**

The Quilting Path: A Guide to Spiritual Discovery through Fabric, Thread and Kabbalah *by Louise Silk*
Explores how to cultivate personal growth through quilt making.
7 x 9, 192 pp, b/w photos and illus., Quality PB, 978-1-59473-206-5 **$16.99**

The Scrapbooking Journey: A Hands-On Guide to Spiritual Discovery *by Cory Richardson-Lauve; Foreword by Stacy Julian* Reveals how this craft can become a practice used to deepen and shape your life.
7 x 9, 176 pp, 8-page color insert, plus b/w photos, Quality PB, 978-1-59473-216-4 **$18.99**

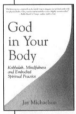

The Soulwork of Clay: A Hands-On Approach to Spirituality
by Marjory Zoet Bankson; Photos by Peter Bankson
Takes you through the seven-step process of making clay into a pot, drawing parallels at each stage to the process of spiritual growth.
7 x 9, 192 pp, b/w photos, Quality PB, 978-1-59473-249-2 **$16.99**

Kabbalah / Enneagram
(Books from Jewish Lights Publishing, SkyLight Paths' sister imprint)

Cast in God's Image: Discover Your Personality Type Using the Enneagram and Kabbalah
by Rabbi Howard A. Addison, PhD 7 x 9, 176 pp, Quality PB, 978-1-58023-124-4 **$16.95**

Ehyeh: A Kabbalah for Tomorrow *by Rabbi Arthur Green, PhD*
6 x 9, 224 pp, Quality PB, 978-1-58023-213-5 **$18.99**

The Enneagram and Kabbalah, 2nd Edition: Reading Your Soul
by Rabbi Howard A. Addison, PhD 6 x 9, 192 pp, Quality PB, 978-1-58023-229-6 **$16.99**

The Gift of Kabbalah: Discovering the Secrets of Heaven, Renewing Your Life on Earth
by Tamar Frankiel, PhD 6 x 9, 256 pp, Quality PB, 978-1-58023-141-1 **$16.95**

God in Your Body: Kabbalah, Mindfulness and Embodied Spiritual Practice
by Jay Michaelson 6 x 9, 272 pp, Quality PB, 978-1-58023-304-0 **$18.99**

Jewish Mysticism and the Spiritual Life: Classical Texts, Contemporary Reflections
Edited by Dr. Lawrence Fine, Dr. Eitan Fishbane and Rabbi Or N. Rose
6 x 9, 256 pp, HC, 978-1-58023-434-4 **$24.99**

Kabbalah: A Brief Introduction for Christians
by Tamar Frankiel, PhD 5½ x 8½, 208 pp, Quality PB, 978-1-58023-303-3 **$16.99**

Zohar: Annotated & Explained *Translation & Annotation by Daniel C. Matt; Foreword by Andrew Harvey* 5½ x 8½, 176 pp, Quality PB, 978-1-893361-51-5 **$15.99**

Spiritual Practice

Fly Fishing—The Sacred Art: Casting a Fly as a Spiritual Practice
by Rabbi Eric Eisenkramer and Rev. Michael Attas, MD
Illuminates what fly fishing can teach you about reflection, awe and wonder; the
benefits of solitude; the blessing of community and the search for the Divine.
5½ x 8½, 192 pp (est), Quality PB, 978-1-59473-299-7 **$16.99**

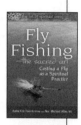

Lectio Divina—The Sacred Art: Transforming Words & Images into
Heart-Centered Prayer *by Christine Valters Paintner, PhD*
Expands the practice of sacred reading beyond scriptural texts and makes it acces-
sible in contemporary life. 5½ x 8½, 192 pp (est), Quality PB, 978-1-59473-300-0 **$16.99**

Haiku—The Sacred Art: A Spiritual Practice in Three Lines
by Margaret D. McGee 5½ x 8½, 192 pp, Quality PB, 978-1-59473-269-0 **$16.99**

Dance—The Sacred Art: The Joy of Movement as a Spiritual Practice
by Cynthia Winton-Henry 5½ x 8½, 224 pp, Quality PB, 978-1-59473-268-3 **$16.99**

Spiritual Adventures in the Snow: Skiing & Snowboarding as Renewal for Your
Soul *by Dr. Marcia McFee and Rev. Karen Foster; Foreword by Paul Arthur*
5½ x 8½, 208 pp, Quality PB, 978-1-59473-270-6 **$16.99**

Divining the Body: Reclaim the Holiness of Your Physical Self *by Jan Phillips*
8 x 8, 256 pp, Quality PB, 978-1-59473-080-1 **$16.99**

Everyday Herbs in Spiritual Life: A Guide to Many Practices
by Michael J. Caduto; Foreword by Rosemary Gladstar
7 x 9, 208 pp, 20+ b/w illus., Quality PB, 978-1-59473-174-7 **$16.99**

Giving—The Sacred Art: Creating a Lifestyle of Generosity
by Lauren Tyler Wright 5½ x 8½, 208 pp, Quality PB, 978-1-59473-224-9 **$16.99**

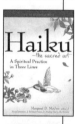

Hospitality—The Sacred Art: Discovering the Hidden Spiritual Power of Invitation
and Welcome *by Rev. Nanette Sawyer; Foreword by Rev. Dirk Ficca*
5½ x 8½, 208 pp, Quality PB, 978-1-59473-228-7 **$16.99**

Labyrinths from the Outside In: Walking to Spiritual Insight—A Beginner's Guide
by Donna Schaper and Carole Ann Camp
6 x 9, 208 pp, b/w illus. and photos, Quality PB, 978-1-893361-18-8 **$16.95**

Practicing the Sacred Art of Listening: A Guide to Enrich Your Relationships and
Kindle Your Spiritual Life *by Kay Lindahl* 8 x 8, 176 pp, Quality PB, 978-1-893361-85-0
$16.95

Recovery—The Sacred Art: The Twelve Steps as Spiritual Practice *by Rami Shapiro;
Foreword by Joan Borysenko, PhD* 5½ x 8½, 240 pp, Quality PB, 978-1-59473-259-1 **$16.99**

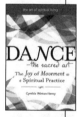

Running—The Sacred Art: Preparing to Practice *by Dr. Warren A. Kay; Foreword by
Kristin Armstrong* 5½ x 8½, 160 pp, Quality PB, 978-1-59473-227-0 **$16.99**

The Sacred Art of Chant: Preparing to Practice
by Ana Hernández 5¼ x 8½, 192 pp, Quality PB, 978-1-59473-036-8 **$15.99**

The Sacred Art of Fasting: Preparing to Practice
by Thomas Ryan, CSP 5½ x 8½, 192 pp, Quality PB, 978-1-59473-078-8 **$15.99**

The Sacred Art of Forgiveness: Forgiving Ourselves and Others through God's Grace
by Marcia Ford 8 x 8, 176 pp, Quality PB, 978-1-59473-175-4 **$18.99**

The Sacred Art of Listening: Forty Reflections for Cultivating a Spiritual Practice
by Kay Lindahl; Illus. by Amy Schnapper 8 x 8, 160 pp, b/w illus., Quality PB, 978-1-893361-44-7 **$16.99**

The Sacred Art of Lovingkindness: Preparing to Practice
by Rabbi Rami Shapiro; Foreword by Marcia Ford 5½ x 8½, 176 pp, Quality PB, 978-1-59473-151-8 **$16.99**

Sacred Attention: A Spiritual Practice for Finding God in the Moment
by Margaret D. McGee 6 x 9, 144 pp, Quality PB, 978-1-59473-291-1 **$16.99**

Soul Fire: Accessing Your Creativity
by Thomas Ryan, CSP 6 x 9, 160 pp, Quality PB, 978-1-59473-243-0 **$16.99**

Thanking & Blessing—The Sacred Art: Spiritual Vitality through Gratefulness
by Jay Marshall, PhD; Foreword by Philip Gulley 5½ x 8½, 176 pp, Quality PB, 978-1-59473-231-7
$16.99

Sacred Texts—SkyLight Illuminations Series

Offers today's spiritual seeker an enjoyable entry into the great classic texts of the world's spiritual traditions. Each classic is presented in an accessible translation, with facing pages of guided commentary from experts, giving you the keys you need to understand the history, context and meaning of the text.

CHRISTIANITY

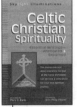

Celtic Christian Spirituality: Essential Writings—Annotated & Explained
Annotation by Mary C. Earle; Foreword by John Philip Newell
Explores how the writings of this lively tradition embody the gospel.
5½ x 8½, 176 pp (est), Quality PB, 978-1-59473-302-4 **$16.99**

The End of Days: Essential Selections from Apocalyptic Texts—
Annotated & Explained *Annotation by Robert G. Clouse, PhD*
Helps you understand the complex Christian visions of the end of the world.
5½ x 8½, 224 pp, Quality PB, 978-1-59473-170-9 **$16.99**

The Hidden Gospel of Matthew: Annotated & Explained
Translation & Annotation by Ron Miller Discover the words and events that have the strongest connection to the historical Jesus.
5½ x 8½, 272 pp, Quality PB, 978-1-59473-038-2 **$16.99**

The Infancy Gospels of Jesus: Apocryphal Tales from the Childhoods of Mary and Jesus—Annotated & Explained
Translation & Annotation by Stevan Davies; Foreword by A. Edward Siecienski, PhD
A startling presentation of the early lives of Mary, Jesus and other biblical figures that will amuse and surprise you. 5½ x 8½, 176 pp, Quality PB, 978-1-59473-258-4 **$16.99**

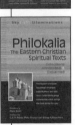

The Lost Sayings of Jesus: Teachings from Ancient Christian, Jewish, Gnostic and Islamic Sources—Annotated & Explained
Translation & Annotation by Andrew Phillip Smith; Foreword by Stephan A. Hoeller
This collection of more than three hundred sayings depicts Jesus as a Wisdom teacher who speaks to people of all faiths as a mystic and spiritual master.
5½ x 8½, 240 pp, Quality PB, 978-1-59473-172-3 **$16.99**

Philokalia: The Eastern Christian Spiritual Texts—Selections Annotated & Explained *Annotation by Allyne Smith; Translation by G. E. H. Palmer, Phillip Sherrard and Bishop Kallistos Ware*
The first approachable introduction to the wisdom of the Philokalia, the classic text of Eastern Christian spirituality. 5½ x 8½, 240 pp, Quality PB, 978-1-59473-103-7 **$16.99**

The Sacred Writings of Paul: Selections Annotated & Explained
Translation & Annotation by Ron Miller Leads you into the exciting immediacy of Paul's teachings. 5½ x 8½, 224 pp, Quality PB, 978-1-59473-213-3 **$16.99**

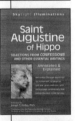

Saint Augustine of Hippo: Selections from *Confessions* and Other Essential Writings—Annotated & Explained
Annotation by Joseph T. Kelley, PhD; Translation by the Augustinian Heritage Institute
Provides insight into the mind and heart of this foundational Christian figure.
5½ x 8½, 272 pp, Quality PB, 978-1-59473-282-9 **$16.99**

St. Ignatius Loyola—The Spiritual Writings: Selections Annotated & Explained *Annotation by Mark Mossa, SJ*
Draws from contemporary translations of original texts focusing on the practical mysticism of Ignatius of Loyola. 5½ x 8½, 224 pp (est), Quality PB, 978-1-59473-301-7 **$16.99**

Sex Texts from the Bible: Selections Annotated & Explained
Translation & Annotation by Teresa J. Hornsby; Foreword by Amy-Jill Levine
Demystifies the Bible's ideas on gender roles, marriage, sexual orientation, virginity, lust and sexual pleasure. 5½ x 8½, 208 pp, Quality PB, 978-1-59473-217-1 **$16.99**

CHRISTIANITY—continued

Spiritual Writings on Mary: Annotated & Explained
Annotation by Mary Ford-Grabowsky; Foreword by Andrew Harvey
Examines the role of Mary, the mother of Jesus, as a source of inspiration in
history and in life today. 5½ x 8½, 288 pp, Quality PB, 978-1-59473-001-6 **$16.99**

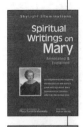

The Way of a Pilgrim: The Jesus Prayer Journey—Annotated & Explained
Translation & Annotation by Gleb Pokrovsky; Foreword by Andrew Harvey
A classic of Russian Orthodox spirituality.
5½ x 8½, 160 pp, Illus., Quality PB, 978-1-893361-31-7 **$14.95**

GNOSTICISM

Gnostic Writings on the Soul: Annotated & Explained
Translation & Annotation by Andrew Phillip Smith; Foreword by Stephan A. Hoeller
Reveals the inspiring ways your soul can remember and return to its unique,
divine purpose. 5½ x 8½, 144 pp, Quality PB, 978-1-59473-220-1 **$16.99**

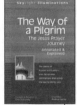

The Gospel of Philip: Annotated & Explained
Translation & Annotation by Andrew Phillip Smith; Foreword by Stevan Davies
Reveals otherwise unrecorded sayings of Jesus and fragments of Gnostic mythology.
5½ x 8½, 160 pp, Quality PB, 978-1-59473-111-2 **$16.99**

The Gospel of Thomas: Annotated & Explained
Translation & Annotation by Stevan Davies; Foreword by Andrew Harvey
Sheds new light on the origins of Christianity and portrays Jesus as a wisdom-loving sage.
5½ x 8½, 192 pp, Quality PB, 978-1-893361-45-4 **$16.99**

The Secret Book of John: The Gnostic Gospel—Annotated & Explained
Translation & Annotation by Stevan Davies The most significant and influential text of
the ancient Gnostic religion. 5½ x 8½, 208 pp, Quality PB, 978-1-59473-082-5 **$16.99**

JUDAISM

The Divine Feminine in Biblical Wisdom Literature
Selections Annotated & Explained
Translation & Annotation by Rabbi Rami Shapiro; Foreword by Rev. Cynthia Bourgeault, PhD
Uses the Hebrew Bible and Wisdom literature to explain Sophia's way of wisdom
and illustrate Her creative energy. 5½ x 8½, 240 pp, Quality PB, 978-1-59473-109-9 **$16.99**

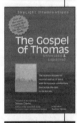

Ecclesiastes: Annotated & Explained
Translation & Annotation by Rabbi Rami Shapiro; Foreword by Rev. Barbara Cawthorne Crafton
A timeless teaching on living well amid uncertainty and insecurity.
5½ x 8½, 160 pp, Quality PB, 978-1-59473-287-4 **$16.99**

Ethics of the Sages: Pirke Avot—Annotated & Explained
Translation & Annotation by Rabbi Rami Shapiro Clarifies the ethical teachings of the
early Rabbis. 5½ x 8½, 192 pp, Quality PB, 978-1-59473-207-2 **$16.99**

Hasidic Tales: Annotated & Explained
Translation & Annotation by Rabbi Rami Shapiro; Foreword by Andrew Harvey
Introduces the legendary tales of the impassioned Hasidic rabbis, presenting them as
stories rather than as parables. 5½ x 8½, 240 pp, Quality PB, 978-1-893361-86-7 **$16.95**

The Hebrew Prophets: Selections Annotated & Explained
Translation & Annotation by Rabbi Rami Shapiro; Foreword by Rabbi Zalman M. Schachter-Shalomi
5½ x 8½, 224 pp, Quality PB, 978-1-59473-037-5 **$16.99**

Tanya, the Masterpiece of Hasidic Wisdom: Selections Annotated &
Explained *Translation & Annotation by Rabbi Rami Shapiro; Foreword by Rabbi Zalman M.
Schachter-Shalomi* Clarifies one of the most powerful and potentially transforma-
tive books of Jewish wisdom. 5½ x 8½, 240 pp, Quality PB, 978-1-59473-275-1 **$16.99**

Zohar: Annotated & Explained *Translation & Annotation by Daniel C. Matt;
Foreword by Andrew Harvey* The canonical text of Jewish mystical tradition.
5½ x 8½, 176 pp, Quality PB, 978-1-893361-51-5 **$15.99**

Sacred Texts—continued

ISLAM

Ghazali on the Principles of Islamic Spirituality

Selections from *Forty Foundations of Religion*—Annotated & Explained
Translation & Annotation by Aaron Spevack, PhD
Makes the core message of this influential spiritual master relevant to anyone seeking a balanced understanding of Islam.
5½ x 8½, 208 pp (est), Quality PB, 978-1-59473-284-3 **$16.99**

The Qur'an and Sayings of Prophet Muhammad

Selections Annotated & Explained
Annotation by Sohaib N. Sultan; Translation by Yusuf Ali, Revised by Sohaib N. Sultan; Foreword by Jane I. Smith
Presents the foundational wisdom of Islam in an easy-to-use format.
5½ x 8½, 256 pp, Quality PB, 978-1-59473-222-5 **$16.99**

Rumi and Islam: Selections from His Stories, Poems, and Discourses—

Annotated & Explained *Translation & Annotation by Ibrahim Gamard*
Focuses on Rumi's place within the Sufi tradition of Islam, providing insight into the mystical side of the religion.
5½ x 8½, 240 pp, Quality PB, 978-1-59473-002-3 **$15.95**

EASTERN RELIGIONS

The Art of War—Spirituality for Conflict: Annotated & Explained

by Sun Tzu; *Annotation by Thomas Huynh; Translation by Thomas Huynh and the Editors at Sonshi.com; Foreword by Marc Benioff; Preface by Thomas Cleary*
Highlights principles that encourage a perceptive and spiritual approach to conflict.
5½ x 8½, 256 pp, Quality PB, 978-1-59473-244-7 **$16.99**

Bhagavad Gita: Annotated & Explained

Translation by Shri Purohit Swami; Annotation by Kendra Crossen Burroughs; Foreword by Andrew Harvey
Presents the classic text's teachings—with no previous knowledge of Hinduism required.
5½ x 8½, 192 pp, Quality PB, 978-1-893361-28-7 **$16.95**

Chuang-tzu: The Tao of Perfect Happiness—Selections Annotated & Explained

Translation & Annotation by Livia Kohn, PhD
Presents Taoism's central message of reverence for the "Way" of the natural world.
5½ x 8½, 240 pp, Quality PB, 978-1-59473-296-6 **$16.99**

Confucius, the *Analects:* The Path of the Sage—Selections Annotated &

Explained *Annotation by Rodney L Taylor, PhD; Translation by James Legge, Revised by Rodney L Taylor, PhD* Explores the ethical and spiritual meaning behind the Confucian way of learning and self-cultivation.
5½ x 8½, 176 pp (est), Quality PB, 978-1-59473-306-2 **$16.99**

Dhammapada: Annotated & Explained

Translation by Max Müller, revised by Jack Maguire; Annotation by Jack Maguire; Foreword by Andrew Harvey Contains all of Buddhism's key teachings, plus commentary that explains all the names, terms and references.
5½ x 8½, 160 pp, b/w photos, Quality PB, 978-1-893361-42-3 **$14.95**

Selections from the Gospel of Sri Ramakrishna: Annotated & Explained

Translation by Swami Nikhilananda; Annotation by Kendra Crossen Burroughs; Foreword by Andrew Harvey Introduces the fascinating world of the Indian mystic and the universal appeal of his message.
5½ x 8½, 240 pp, b/w photos, Quality PB, 978-1-893361-46-1 **$16.95**

Tao Te Ching: Annotated & Explained

Translation & Annotation by Derek Lin; Foreword by Lama Surya Das
Introduces an Eastern classic in an accessible, poetic and completely original way.
5½ x 8½, 208 pp, Quality PB, 978-1-59473-204-1 **$16.99**

Sacred Texts—continued

MORMONISM

The Book of Mormon: Selections Annotated & Explained
Annotation by Jana Riess; Foreword by Phyllis Tickle Explores the sacred epic that is cherished by more than twelve million members of the LDS church as the keystone of their faith. 5½ x 8½, 272 pp, Quality PB, 978-1-59473-076-4 **$16.99**

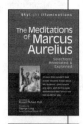

NATIVE AMERICAN

Native American Stories of the Sacred: Annotated & Explained
Retold & Annotated by Evan T. Pritchard These teaching tales contain elegantly simple illustrations of time-honored truths. 5½ x 8½, 272 pp, Quality PB, 978-1-59473-112-9 **$16.99**

STOICISM

The Meditations of Marcus Aurelius: Selections Annotated & Explained *Annotation by Russell McNeil, PhD; Translation by George Long, revised by Russell McNeil, PhD* Ancient Stoic wisdom that speaks vibrantly today about life, business, government and spirit. 5½ x 8½, 288 pp, Quality PB, 978-1-59473-236-2 **$16.99**

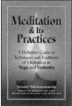

Hinduism / Vedanta

The Four Yogas: A Guide to the Spiritual Paths of Action, Devotion, Meditation and Knowledge *by Swami Adiswarananda*
6 x 9, 320 pp, Quality PB, 978-1-59473-223-2 **$19.99**; HC, 978-1-59473-143-3 **$29.99**

Meditation & Its Practices: A Definitive Guide to Techniques and Traditions of Meditation in Yoga and Vedanta *by Swami Adiswarananda* 6 x 9, 504 pp, Quality PB, 978-1-59473-105-1 **$24.99**

The Spiritual Quest and the Way of Yoga: The Goal, the Journey and the Milestones *by Swami Adiswarananda* 6 x 9, 288 pp, HC, 978-1-59473-113-6 **$29.99**

Sri Ramakrishna, the Face of Silence
by Swami Nikhilananda and Dhan Gopal Mukerji; Edited with an Introduction by Swami Adiswarananda; Foreword by Dhan Gopal Mukerji II 6 x 9, 352 pp, Quality PB, 978-1-59473-233-1 **$21.99**

Sri Sarada Devi, The Holy Mother: Her Teachings and Conversations
Translated with Notes by Swami Nikhilananda; Edited with an Introduction by Swami Adiswarananda
6 x 9, 288 pp, HC, 978-1-59473-070-2 **$29.99**

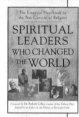

The Vedanta Way to Peace and Happiness *by Swami Adiswarananda*
6 x 9, 240 pp, Quality PB, 978-1-59473-180-8 **$18.99**; HC, 978-1-59473-034-4 **$29.99**

Vivekananda, World Teacher: His Teachings on the Spiritual Unity of Humankind
Edited and with an Introduction by Swami Adiswarananda
6 x 9, 272 pp, Quality PB, 978-1-59473-210-2 **$21.99**

Sikhism

The First Sikh Spiritual Master: Timeless Wisdom from the Life and Teachings of Guru Nanak *by Harish Dhillon* 6 x 9, 192 pp, Quality PB, 978-1-59473-209-6 **$16.99**

Spiritual Biography

Spiritual Leaders Who Changed the World
The Essential Handbook to the Past Century of Religion
Edited by Ira Rifkin and the Editors at SkyLight Paths; Foreword by Dr. Robert Coles
An invaluable reference to the most important spiritual leaders of the past 100 years.
6 x 9, 304 pp, b/w photos, Quality PB, 978-1-59473-241-6 **$18.99**

Mahatma Gandhi: His Life and Ideas *by Charles F. Andrews; Foreword by Dr. Arun Gandhi* Examines the religious ideas and political dynamics that influenced the birth of the peaceful resistance movement. 6 x 9, 336 pp, b/w photos, Quality PB, 978-1-893361-89-8 **$18.95**

Bede Griffiths: An Introduction to His Interspiritual Thought
by Wayne Teasdale The first study of his contemplative experience and thought, exploring the intersection of Hinduism and Christianity.
6 x 9, 288 pp, Quality PB, 978-1-893361-77-5 **$18.95**

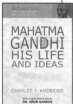

About SKYLIGHT PATHS Publishing

SkyLight Paths Publishing is creating a place where people of different spiritual traditions come together for challenge and inspiration, a place where we can help each other understand the mystery that lies at the heart of our existence.

Through spirituality, our religious beliefs are increasingly becoming a part of our lives—rather than *apart* from our lives. While many of us may be more interested than ever in spiritual growth, we may be less firmly planted in traditional religion. Yet, we do want to deepen our relationship to the sacred, to learn from our own as well as from other faith traditions, and to practice in new ways.

SkyLight Paths sees both believers and seekers as a community that increasingly transcends traditional boundaries of religion and denomination—people wanting to learn from each other, *walking together, finding the way.*

For your information and convenience, at the back of this book we have provided a list of other SkyLight Paths books you might find interesting and useful. They cover the following subjects:

Buddhism / Zen	Global Spiritual	Monasticism
Catholicism	Perspectives	Mysticism
Children's Books	Gnosticism	Poetry
Christianity	Hinduism /	Prayer
Comparative	Vedanta	Religious Etiquette
Religion	Inspiration	Retirement
Current Events	Islam / Sufism	Spiritual Biography
Earth-Based	Judaism	Spiritual Direction
Spirituality	Kabbalah	Spirituality
Enneagram	Meditation	Women's Interest
	Midrash Fiction	Worship